WRITERS AND THEIR WORK

ISOBEL ARMSTRONG
General Editor

BRYAN LOUGHREY
Advisory Editor

Jean Rhys

JEAN RHYS

Jean
Rhys

Helen Carr

Northcote House

in association with
The British Council

Acknowledgements

The author and the publishers gratefully
acknowledge Penguin Books Limited for
permission to quote from the Penguin editions of
the works of Jean Rhys

First published in 1996 by Northcote House Publishers Ltd, Plymbridge House,
Estover Road, Plymouth PL6 7PZ, United Kingdom.
Tel: (01752) 735251. Fax: (01752) 695699.

British Library Cataloguing-in-Publication Data
A catalogue record for this book is available from the British Library

ISBN 0 7463 0717 9

Typeset by PDQ Typesetting, Newcastle-Under-Lyme
Printed and bound in the United Kingdom by BPC Wheatons Ltd, Exeter

Contents

Biographical Outline

1890	Born Ella Gwendoline Rees Williams on 24 August in Roseau, Dominica, West Indies, to a Creole mother of Scottish and Irish descent, and to a Welsh doctor father.
1907	Comes to England, to the Perse School for Girls in Cambridge.
1909	Two terms at the Academy of Dramatic Art: leaves to become a chorus-girl, under the names, at various times of Vivien, Emma or Ella Gray.
1910	First affair with Launcelot Hugh Smith, twenty years her senior.
1912	Hugh Smith breaks off the affair.
1919	Goes to Holland to marry Jean Lenglet, a Dutch-French poet and journalist. They move to Paris.
1922	Her son William dies at the age of three weeks. They move to Vienna.
1922	They return to Paris. Her daughter Maryvonne is born.
1924	Meets Ford Madox Ford, who encourages her writing. Lenglet is imprisoned for currency irregularities. She becomes Ford's mistress. 'Vienne', her first published story appears in the *transatlantic review*, edited by Ford, under the name Jean Rhys.
1927	*The Left Bank and Other Stories* published in Britain and the USA. Leslie Tilden Smith becomes her literary agent.
1928	*Postures* (i.e. *Quartet*) published in Britain. She and Tilden Smith start living together in London.
1929	*Quartet* published in the USA.
1930	*After Leaving Mr Mackenzie* published in Britain.
1931	*After Leaving Mr Mackenzie* published in the USA.
1933	Rhys and Lenglet are divorced.

1934	*Voyage in the Dark* published in Britain. She and Tilden Smith marry.
1935	*Voyage in the Dark* published in the USA.
1936	Visits Dominica with Tilden Smith.
1937	Pays the visit to Paris on which she begins *Good Morning, Midnight*.
1939	*Good Morning, Midnight* published in Britain.
1945	Leslie Tilden Smith dies. Daughter Maryvonne, who had worked with the Dutch Resistance during the war, marries.
1946	Rhys and Max Hamer start living together. They move to Hamer's house in Beckenham.
1947	She and Hamer marry.
1948	Maryvonne has a baby girl, Ellen Ruth.
1949	Rhys spends about five days in Holloway Prison. 'Rediscovered' by Selma Vaz Dias through an advertisement in the *New Statesman*.
1950	Hamer imprisoned for minor fraud.
1951-2	Rhys lives by herself for about nine months near Maidstone at the Ropemakers Arms. Part of the diary she kept there was later published in *Smile Please*.
1952	Hamer released.
1955	They move to Cornwall.
1957	Adaptation of *Good Morning, Midnight* broadcast by the BBC. Rhys signs a contract with Andre Deutsch for the novel which was to become *Wide Sargasso Sea*. From now on she has much more encouragement and friendship, particularly from Diana Athill of Andre Deutsch, Francis Wyndham and Diana Melly.
1960	They move to Cheriton Fitzpaine in Devon. 'Till September, Petronella' and 'The Day They Burned the Books' published in the *London Magazine*.
1966	Hamer dies. *Wide Sargasso Sea* published in Britain, winning the W. H. Smith Prize.
1967	*Voyage in the Dark* and *Good Morning, Midnight* reissued in Britain. *Wide Sargasso Sea* published in the USA.
1968	*Tigers are Better-Looking* (collection of short stories including some from *The Left Bank*) published in Britain. *Voyage in the Dark* reissued in the USA.
1969	'Temps Perdi' and 'I Spy a Stranger' published in *Penguin*

	Modern Stories. *Quartet* and *After Leaving Mr Mackenzie* reissued in Britain.
1970	*Good Morning, Midnight* published in the USA.
1971	*Quartet* reissued in the USA.
1972	*After Leaving Mr Mackenzie* reissued in the USA.
1974	*Tigers are Better-Looking* published in the USA.
1975	*My Day*, a collection of three autobiographical pieces, published in the USA.
1976	*Sleep It Off Lady* (short stories) published in Britain and the USA.
1979	Jean Rhys dies. *Smile Please* (autobiography) published posthumously in Britain and the USA.

Abbreviations and References

(Page numbers with these abbreviations refer to the Penguin editions of Rhys's works except for *TP*.)

Note on Ellipses

Jean Rhys uses ellipses very frequently, so in order to distinguish between her ellipses and those which indicate something has been omitted, in quotations from her texts my ellipses are in brackets: i.e. [. . .]. In quotations from other sources, the ellipses are always mine.

Introduction

In 1949 Jean Rhys was living in Beckenham, Kent, already no longer a separate town, but absorbed into Greater London. She always disliked England, cold in climate and in soul as she had felt it to be ever since she first arrived from the West Indies in 1907, but the stolid and unyielding respectability of suburban Beckenham came to discomfit her more than anywhere else. Jean Rhys discomfited Beckenham too: when she first arrived she was 'living in sin', as local gossip quickly guessed and doubtless put it. She got drunk, quarrelled with her neighbours, and appeared in court nine times over two years on charges ranging from throwing a brick through the window of a neighbour whose dog had (allegedly) killed her cats, to biting a policeman. She had published nothing since her fourth novel, *Good Morning, Midnight*, in 1939, aptly named, as she later commented, to greet the war (JRL, 97). Yet through all the terror of the Blitz, and the unexpected and devastating death of her second husband in 1945, she went on writing, short stories that were not to be published till many years later, and early versions of the book that was to become *Wide Sargasso Sea*. But by the autumn of 1949 she became too discouraged: her third (now legal) marriage was under stress, and her husband, she suspected correctly, was heading for financial and personal disaster. Although he had owned the house in Beckenham some time before he moved her in, it was in terrible repair and very damp. She had no friends nearby, and had lost touch with her London literary contacts. She had spent some harrowing and humiliating days in Holloway, under psychiatric observation, after berating the magistrate at her latest trial. 'He asked me if I had anything to say. So I said it', she wrote to her friend Peggy Kirkcaldy (CA, 446). She was desperate for encouragement but found none in 'damp and bloody' 'God-forsaken' Beckenham (JRL, 59). A local court doctor predictably pronounced her a hysteric: it seemed 'rather odd', the *Beckenham Journal* reported that she had commented, 'to say that she was hysterical because she wrote books. It was rather English.'[1] For the first time in her life, she wrote to Peggy, she lost the desire to write (JRL, 55).

It was at this point that the most well-known event of Jean Rhys's life occurred. She was 'rediscovered'. The actress Selma Vaz Dias wanted to turn *Good Morning, Midnight* into a radio play, and needed Jean Rhys's permission. Unable to trace her, and told by many that Rhys was probably dead, she advertised in the *New Statesman* on 5 November for information. Jean Rhys saw the advertisement and replied the same day. The problem was not just that 'Jean Rhys' was a pseudonym, but the remarriage. Vaz Dias had been looking for 'Mrs Tilden Smith': if only she had realized, regular information about 'Ella Gwendolen Hamer (56) a writer' was appearing in the law reports of the South London press (CA, 442).

It was not until 1957 that the BBC were to broadcast the play, and not until 1966 that Rhys's last and most famous novel, *Wide Sargasso Sea* was published. It was in fact a very slow and uneven literary resurrection. Vaz Dias lost touch with Jean Rhys again in 1953. By then Rhys's husband had come out of prison after serving two years for minor fraud: he had lost his job and pension, and they were living in dire poverty, mainly on hand-outs from reluctant relatives. In 1956 Vaz Dias persuaded the BBC to advertise once more, though this time only for Rhys's address. With an eye for publicity, Vaz Dias wrote the story up for the *Radio Times*, mentioning only the second advertisement and giving promise of the new novel, thus bestowing on the story the fairy-tale quality with which it is now retold – Rhys as Sleeping Beauty to Vaz Dias's Prince. (In some versions, with more a conventionally gendered narrative, the role of Prince is transferred to Francis Wyndham, a long-time admirer of her work, who did indeed play an important part in encouraging Rhys to finish *Wide Sargasso Sea*, but was in fact only alerted to her whereabouts by Vaz Dias's article.) Yet it was the earlier awakening in 1949 that was the significant one: Vaz Dias's action dissolved that short-lived paralysis of will. A month after replying to that first advertisement Jean Rhys was saying, 'I could write something else given a little peace, a little sympathy and all those elusive things...It's a thousand to one chance I know. Nevertheless I will try...because it's woken up my desire to write' (JRL, 64). And whatever problems she may have had in completing work after that (she summed them up succinctly in 1957 as 'No privacy, No cash, No security, No resilience, No youth, No desk to write on, No table even. No one who understands' (CA, 476) she never again seems to have lost the wish to write.

In 1949, however, her neighbours refused to be impressed. 'My bitter enemy next door' (owner of the cat-molesting dog), she wrote to Peggy, 'is now telling everybody very loud and clear that I'm an impostor "impersonating a dead writer called Jean Rhys"'. She added, as a postscript, 'It's a weird feeling being told you are impersonating yourself. Rather nightmarish. You think; perhaps I am.' (JRL, 64) That postscript goes to the heart of Jean Rhys's anxieties and of her writing. The vulnerability, inventedness and multiplicity of identity are constant and central themes in Jean Rhys's writing: who am I? what am I? what are they making of me? are questions that in different ways all her heroines try to answer, not with much satisfaction... 'I often wonder who I am and where is my country and where do I belong and why was I ever born at all', as Antoinette says in *Wide Sargasso Sea* (*WSS* 85). No wonder, perhaps, Rhys's enemy's words struck home. The nightmare (which she shared with Sartre and Beckett) of a self defined by other people, the oddly disconcerting change of pronoun in that last sentence, which opens up the gap between the self ('you think') which searches for self-definition, and the self ('perhaps I am') who is uncertainly defined: these shifts and breaks and fears infuse all her fictional and autobiographical explorations. 'You think: perhaps I am': it could be read appropriately enough as Jean Rhys's sceptical, shaky, post-Enlightenment reworking of the seamlessly confident Cartesian self, the bold, resolute ego which marches on proclaiming, I think, therefore I am.

What led to Jean Rhys's preoccupation with the precariousness and dangers of identity? Was it her experience as a colonial? As a woman? Her ambiguous, déclassé status in a still rigidly hierarchical system? Her intellectual response to a world whose certainties were gone? I think Rachel Bowlby is right to argue that it would be a mistake to look for one master key to Rhys's work.[2] All those different elements are there. Jean Rhys cannot be considered exclusively as a Caribbean writer, or as a woman writer, a novelist of the demi-monde, or as a modernist. She is all of those, but being all of those, none fit her as unproblematic labels. What I shall want to argue here is that her position, in these different ways, as migrant, marginal, homeless, never, as she says in *Quartet*, 'quite of the fold' (*Q* 12), made it possible for her to write novels which both went to the heart of the prejudices, exclusions and paranoia of the period in which she wrote, and as well explore a dimension of modernist, even postmodernist consciousness that perhaps only appears elsewhere before the Second World War in Kafka's work. In the years after she was 'rediscovered' one of the repeated comments on her work was how far ahead of their time her prewar novels had been. This was often a response to her treatment of sexual relationships, particularly her depiction of women in the shadows of city life and on the underedge of respectability. But her treatment of sexuality is only one of the aspects in which the uncertain, indifferent, discontinuous world of her novels looks so contemporary. Her fiction, dealing as it does with those who belong nowhere, between cultures, between histories, describes an existence which is becoming paradigmatic of late twentieth-century life. As Heidegger said, 'Homelessness is coming to be the destiny of the world', and 'homelessness' is the terrain of Jean Rhys's fiction.[3]

1

Jean Rhys and Her Critics

Yet for a long time Jean Rhys's fiction was seen in much more circumscribed terms: gifted, perhaps; of cultural significance, no; self-absorbed, emphatically so; well executed for a woman, but still women's fiction, with all that implied in limitation of scope and significance. Before the publication of *Wide Sargasso Sea* few readers noticed or commented on her Caribbean origins, so crucially important to her work in multiple ways: not always even then, although the novel is largely set in the West Indies, and refashions the story of the most famous fictional Creole woman, the first Mrs Rochester from *Jane Eyre*. Conversely, for decades the fact that her fiction had first appeared in the context of modernist writing was forgotten or ignored. That her fiction is often very funny, even if certainly tragicomedy rather than comedy, was ignored. Her books were most often read as highly personal accounts of an individual woman's unhappy lot. Like Sylvia Plath, Jean Rhys has suffered from having her life and work read against one another, fused into a myth of feminine distress. It is a myth which has obscured much of the significance and complexity of her writing.

To understand how that myth arose, and why her modernism was forgotten, one needs to go back to the history of her reception as a writer, and to the break between her early reputation and her later fame. There is no doubt that Ford Madox Ford, impresario to so many male writers of modernist fiction, considered her of their camp in his somewhat *de haut en bas* introduction to her first collection of stories, *The Left Bank*, published in 1927. He commended her admirable attention to the exemplary models for Anglo-Saxon modernist prose, Flaubert and Maupassant, and in particular praised with some surprise 'the singular instinct for form possessed by this young lady, an instinct for form being possessed

1

by singularly few writers of English and by almost no English women writers' *(LB* 24–5). Most of those who reviewed her first four novels also identified her with the modern school, comparing her to the Imagist poets, to Hemingway, to Katherine Mansfield[1] – though, unlike Ford, what tended to strike those early reviewers about her as a woman writer was not so much the excellence of her style as her obsession with the more disagreeable aspects of life and womanhood. Her stories of shabby hotels in Paris and drab bedsitting-rooms in London appeared to many of them tales of the underworld rather than of the demi-monde, and her heroines were regularly and unequivocally described as prostitutes. Yet, in spite of some ambivalent critical responses to her work ('we shall have to go far to find another novel so powerfully wrought out of weakness, futility, betrayal, lust and fear' ... 'the sordid little story is written with admirable clarity and economy of language' ... 'the truth about the grotesque and ugly and contemptible side of life could scarcely be told better than it is told here'), she achieved a small audience of appreciative readers.[2]

During Rhys's years of obscurity, however, the slender reputation of her prewar books slipped away. If her work had been found sordid but artistic between the wars, it was – except to a tiny handful – unreadable and unread in the postwar promotion of family life, Little England and the Cold War. The twenties and thirties had been, it is sometimes forgotten, more questioning of sexual mores than the postwar years. In the early fifties Rhys was gloomy about what could be published in England. In 1953 she wrote to Morchard Bishop:

> I read a letter in the Observer last Sunday from some editor – Peter Green – promising to accept any story up to (of) the standard of 'Boule de Suif'.[3] Well I should damned well think he would! [...]
>
> Poor old Boule de Suif. They won't let her rest –
>
> The thing I very much doubt is whether any story seriously glorifying the prostitute and showing up not one but several British housewives to say nothing of two nuns! – their meannesses and cant and spite – would be accepted by the average editor or any editor.
>
> And 'La Maison Tellier?'[4] – Well imagine –
>
> Of course I may be quite wrong. [...] But I do read a lot and have a very definite impression that 'thought control' is on the way and ought to be resisted. But will it be resisted?
>
> Why say as Mr. Green does 'I demand a positive and creative view of life.'?

2

What is that? And why *demand* a view of life. Not his business surely. [...] I do feel rather deeply about this thought control matter. So insidious. And suddenly it's there – Not to be resisted any more. (JRL, 99–100)

Significantly, it was not until 1957, a year after Suez, *Look Back in Anger* and Bill Haley's 'Rock Around the Clock', that, with the country's mood beginning to shift, the BBC agreed finally to broadcast *Good Morning, Midnight*.

Like many modernist writers, Rhys had used her life, in all its painful rawness, as the material from which she formed her fiction. The process of transmutation was always for her a long and arduous struggle, because, she said, 'a novel has to have a shape and life doesn't have any' (*SP* 10). But, though praise for that sense of shape and form continued, when Rhys came back into public view the autobiographical content of her writing was more often read as scarcely mediated confession rather than a problematic starting-point, and her relation to her central characters treated very differently from that of other, and particularly male modernist writers. As Judith Kegan Gardiner has commented:

> When a writer like Joyce or Eliot writes about an alienated man estranged from himself, [such a figure] is read as a portrait of the diminished possibilities of human existence in modern society. When Rhys writes about an alienated woman estranged from herself, critics applaud her perceptive but narrow depiction of female experience and tend to narrow her vision even further by labelling it both pathological and autobiographical.[5]

If she wrote about her own life, it was assumed, it was because that was all she had to write about, not because she had something to say about the kind of world in which such a life could happen. 'To meet [Jean Rhys], I discovered,' wrote one interviewer, 'was to be simultaneously introduced to Sasha, Julia, Marya, Anna, even Mrs Rochester.'[6] It is hard to conceive of an interviewer writing: 'To meet D. H. Lawrence, I discovered, was to be simultaneously introduced to Paul Morel, Birkin, Somers, the Man Who Died, even Lady Chatterley's Lover'.

Simply being a woman writer is of course, as Judith Kegan Gardiner implies, one factor in evoking such a very personalized response, but in Jean Rhys's case there was an additional reason.

3

The years following her belated critical success were those in which confessional writing was very much in vogue. It was after all Al Alvarez, high-priest of the art of psychic extremity, who sealed her reputation by proclaiming her in 1974 'the best living novelist'.[7] In 1927, Ford Madox Ford, to his credit, had recognized the devastating social critique that fuels Rhys's fiction, and saw its link with her alien colonial origins:

> Coming from the Antilles, with a terrifying insight and a terrific – an almost lurid! – passion for stating the case of the underdog, she has let her pen loose on the Left Banks of the Old World – on its gaols, its studios, its salons, its cafes, its criminals, its midinettes – with a bias of admiration for its midinettes and of sympathy for its law-breakers. (*LB* 24)

In the early seventies the fiction was read as the expression solely of Jean Rhys's own experience as an underdog, the unfolding story of the ever sadder fate of the 'Rhys woman', as her heroines became compositely known. For Walter Allen, the character of Antoinette in *Wide Sargasso Sea* summed up

> the nature of the heroine who appears under various names throughout Jean Rhys's fiction...
> She is a young woman... who is hopelessly and helplessly at sea in her relations with men, a passive victim doomed to destruction.[8]

Elgin W. Mellown commenting on this judgement, turned to Jean Rhys's life for confirmation:

> The woman upon whom Rhys centres her attention is indeed always a victim. Stella Bowen [Ford Madox Ford's lover and prototype of Lois in *Quartet*] saw this quality in the novelist herself and described her as being 'cast for the rôle... of the poor, brave and desperate beggar who was doomed to be let down by the bourgeoisie'.[9]

The years between the publication of *Wide Sargasso Sea* and Rhys's death in 1979 saw the beginnings of second-wave feminism, with its considerable impact on the literary media, and the concentration of these critics on the powerlessness of the 'Rhys woman' should perhaps be understood in that context. Rhys and her writing came to be seen, depending on the reader's view of Womens Liberation, as emblematic either of women's oppression or of their self-pity. As with Sylvia Plath, whose early reputation also owed much to Alvarez, and who began to attract wide attention at much the same time as Rhys, interpretations of the work and of the life fused inextricably together. In Plath's case, her poetry was – and often still is – read as preface and key to her suicide. To her sympathizers she is a victim of male brutality, to her detractors the victim of her own neurosis: in either case, her work is her cry of pain. Similarly, Jean Rhys's fiction has been read as the retelling through her heroines of her own melancholy tale of defeat, whether this defeat is judged to be at the hands of callous men or the result of her own apathetic ineptitude. This mythic portrayal of feminine distress has resulted, for both Plath and Rhys, in a blindness to the range and intelligence of their work. In the case of Rhys, it has occluded the crucial political dimension of her work, and also, it must be said, her irony, wit and satire.

Jean Rhys had complained for years about the low esteem in which women writers were held in Britain: not just court doctors who pronounced them hysterics in their 'rather English' way, but the *'damnable'* 'anglo-saxon idea that you can be rude with impunity to any female who has written a book [. . .] You come and have a look out of curiosity and then allow the freak to see what you think of her. It's only done to the more or less unsuccessful and only by anglo-saxons' (JRL, 32). Jean Rhys enjoyed – up to a point – the different kind of gaze that success brought, but she still found herself and her works trapped within female stereotypes. One of my reasons for beginning my account with Jean Rhys in Beckenham 'protesting loudly', as the court reports put it, is to underline the inadequacy of this image of her as a passive, hopeless and helpless victim, from whom her heroines and their bleak lives are cloned. After the publication of *Wide Sargasso Sea*, when she had become a famous literary figure, Jean Rhys found herself again and again depicted, by analogy with her heroines, as oppressed and defeated. It was an image that irritated her considerably: she was frequently interviewed by reporters, whose 'question-and-answer game' she complained in 1978, 'gently pushed' her into her

> predestined role, the role of victim. I have never had any good times, never got my own back, never dared, never worn pretty clothes, never been happy, never known wild hopes or wilder despairs. [. . .] Waiting, I have gone from tyrant to tyrant: each let down worse than the last.[10]

One could argue that she is here complaining of being victimized, even though it is by being portrayed as a victim, but she is also, it must be noted, protesting vigorously against it. Similarly in her fiction: whilst it is true that Rhys wrote of women (and sometimes men) acutely conscious of their lack of power, unsure of how to act, feeling themselves silenced or unheard, what she does in writing her novels is to assert the right and power to speak on their behalf. Writing a novel for a perfectionist like Jean Rhys took enormous energy and stamina: nothing passive or defeated about it at all. Rhys may have been, as Bowen suggests, let down by the bourgeoisie (in Beckenham they must have felt it was mutual) but she saved herself. In 1952, while waiting for her second husband to come out of prison, she wrote in her diary:

> I must write. If I stop writing my life will have been an abject failure. It is that already to other people. But it could be an abject failure to myself. I will not have earned death. (*SP* 163)

She did go on writing: her life was not a failure. In her battles with depression, damp and destitution, it was, in its way, heroic.

'Passive victim' is, in any case, as inadequate a description for her heroines as for Jean Rhys herself, and not only because she shows them frequently as angry and as badly behaved as she was. Marya hits Heidler, Anna stubs her cigarette on Walter's hand, Julia makes a scene at her mother's funeral, Antoinette bites her husband and threatens him with a broken rum bottle. Woman as passive victim has been a powerful stereotype, indeed, sexual fantasy, since the eighteenth century, exemplified, as Angela Carter's *The Sadeian Woman* so graphically argues, in de Sade's *Justine*.[11] Jean Rhys's heroines are aware of the lure of that fantasy, but that does not mean that that is all they are. I shall look at this in more detail later, but what I want principally to stress at this point is that the emphasis on the passive victim has made it harder, or less necessary, to acknowledge the intensity of Rhys's attack on social injustice: a victim who is passive is by common consent (as Jean Rhys bitterly noted) to a great extent to blame for her fate. The phrase implies that 'passivity' is an innate characteristic of that particular victim, and not that there could be social, cultural or historical conditions which have driven this 'victim' into an impasse.[12] Again there is a parallel with Plath.

6

Commenting on Stephen Spender's contrast between Plath, whose poetry he alleges is that of 'priestess cultivating her hysteria...completely out of herself', and Wilfred Owen, whose anguished poetry comes out of the exterior evil of the First World War, Jacqueline Rose cites Mary Ellmann's objection to this 'removal of the woman from history, this turning-into-herself of all historical and literary process'. Rose adds: 'I would go further, and suggest that it is basic to this fantasmatic scenario that the woman becomes the horror of which she speaks'.[13] So with Rhys: the insistence that her fiction tells the story of the fantasmatic willing, passive, masochistic victim, means that Jean Rhys/the heroine herself becomes the source and origin of her power-lessness. The anger against injustice and hypocrisy behind Rhys's 'terrific – almost lurid! – passion for stating the case of the underdog' disappears from view.

There was another element in the reluctance of critics to consider Rhys as a modernist. Modernism was above all a self-conscious movement, a literary movement acutely aware of other writers. A woman who 'wrote almost exclusively about herself',[14] as Rhys was so often said to do, was not, it was assumed, in the intellectual class to be considered a modernist. Good at emotion, poor on ideas – that was another of those female stereotypes which stuck to Rhys, even though it was one she had satirized herself in *Good Morning, Midnight*. There René, appalled by Sasha's description of herself as a *Cérébrale*, says in horror:

'Is that your idea of yourself?' [...]
  'It is, certainly.'
  'It's not mine at all. I should have thought you rather stupid. [...] No, no. Don't be vexed. I don't mean stupid. I mean that you feel better than you think.' (*GMM* 135)

In the seventies and beyond, even when Jean Rhys was fêted as a writer, it was very much as a feeling, not a thinking writer: she was intuitive rather than intelligent, a naïve, instinctive, ill-educated genius. That she might be a reader as well as writer, and hence a writer conscious of and influenced by other writers, was hardly considered, even though her most famous book was a reworking of another novel. In this way her reputation has been rather different from that of Plath, whose work, Jacqueline Rose argues, has been read too narrowly in terms of high culture, and her fascination with popular forms ignored. (Rhys's fiction is threaded with allusions to popular songs, popular literature, and the cinema, all of which deserve more attention, but in her work both popular and literary references have been generally neglected.) To many, Plath, the model student with her straight 'A's from Smith and success at Cambridge, was too intellectually ambitious for her own womanly good: to Rhys, on the contrary, ex-chorus girl, ex-model, was ascribed a feminine, superficial approach to literature. The biographical myth, which has made much of Rhys's simultaneously glamorous and contemptible beginnings, has always centred on her sexuality. The Penguin blurb, for example, does not mention she was to be an actress until forced to leave drama-school, but describes her start in the world as 'drift[ing] into a series of hopeless jobs – chorus-girl, mannequin, artist's model'.[15] Hopeless? Such jobs could lead to fame and fortune: in fact probably the kind of professions entered into with more hope than most. What Penguin mean by hopeless is not intellectually respectable, not even really middle-class, jobs which drew on female sexuality and therefore were taken to indicate a lack of female mind. Once more, it is a pattern which Rhys comments on in her fiction: in 'Vienne', Frances complains of the men who 'always disdain[ed] my mind and concentrat[ed] on my body' (*TABL* 205). Jean Rhys's mind has been often disdained, by critics of both sexes. David Plante, for example, in his much-quoted account of her in *Difficult Women*, implies, along with frequent comments on her ill-applied make-up, that Rhys was never a serious reader. Plante only got to know Rhys in her late eighties – he writes as if old age were a tasteless, grotesque vice that she had succumbed to through moral rather than mortal frailty – and it is hard to know what credence to give to the statements he records. She was so old, and he mainly quotes what she said when drunk, and when drunk, she wrote elsewhere, she generally tried to scandalize interviewers rather than inform them. In any case, Plante says he was drunk too, so perhaps his memories may not be reliable: they certainly are suspiciously apt for his misogynist message. And in addition, Jean Rhys was always – young, old, drunk, sober – immensely self-deprecating. However that may be, he says that she told him she could not read Balzac, Proust, Fielding, Trollope, George Eliot, James, Conrad or Joyce. As she quotes Conrad in *After Leaving Mr Mackenzie*, mentions in a letter that she is reading *Turn of the Screw* for the sixth time, has several references to Joyce, and at least one to Proust, that cannot be entirely true.[16] As to modern writers, Plante simply says, grudgingly: 'she knew many modern writers well enough to comment on them', and gives one insubstantial reference to her reading a book by Beckett and thinking him too studied.[17] Plante's memoir has been immensely influential. In 1990, her biographer was still assuming that she had no real contact with contemporary writing or ideas.

> This is one of the most intriguing of all the paradoxes about Jean Rhys, that she knew so little, and wrote only about herself, and yet she managed to write novels which were completely modern, full of feelings, ideas, even literary terms that were absolutely of her time. (CA, 218)

This image of Jean Rhys, the inward-looking chronicler of private pathos, ignorant of literary culture, untutored even if intuiting the tone of her times, has clung as closely as that of the passive victim, in spite of the overwhelming evidence to the contrary in her fiction, her letters, her autobiography and in the testimony of others like Ford and her first husband: all make clear that she read all the time, compulsively, always wanting to know what other writers were about, as the letter to Morchard Bishop which I quoted earlier illustrates. Her fiction is full of references to other fiction and to poetry. She is selective but scarcely narrow – her references in her texts and letters suggest that the pre-twentieth-century writers she draws on most (in addition, of course, to the Brontës) are Shakespeare, the Romantic poets, the French precursors of modernism (Flaubert, Maupassant, Baudelaire, Rimbaud, etc.), and a range of 1890s writers in both French and English. In the twentieth century she read very widely in both English and French, particularly in fiction.[18] As Judith Kegan Gardiner argued in 1982, then very much against the trend, she is a much more literary writer than most critics have granted. Writing on *Good Morning, Midnight*, Gardiner points out that not only is the title a quotation from Emily Dickinson, and the ending a parody of *Ulysses*, but that references to Keats, Rimbaud, Verlaine, Wilde, Anatole France, Woolf and Colette play a significant part in the course of the book.[19] *Wide Sargasso Sea* is not the only one of her works to rewrite other texts: for example, her short story, 'La Grosse Fifi', is, as Coral Ann Howells has pointed out, an ironic reworking of Maupassant's 'Mademoiselle Fifi', her war-time story 'Temps Perdi' ('Temps Perdi', Rhys explains, 'is Creole patois and does not mean, poetically, lost or forgotten time, but, matter-of-factly, wasted time, lost labour', TP 155) is a bleak, postmodern re-examination of the Proustian involuntary memory. Perhaps one reason English critics were slow to recognize the extensive intertextuality within her writing was lack of knowledge of her French sources, but largely, I surmise, it was that they brought with them the assumption that she was, as Alvarez had insisted, completely 'non-intellectual'.[21]

2

Feminist and Postcolonial Approaches to Jean Rhys

Given the sexual prejudice which fuelled this judgement, other feminist critics were slower than one might expect to follow up Judith Kegan Gardiner's suggestions. In fact, although newspaper and magazine articles so often saw the fate of Rhys's heroines in terms of contemporary protests against male domination, feminist academic critics have by no means welcomed her work unequivocally.[1] Feminist criticism in the seventies concentrated either on nineteenth-century or on contemporary feminist writers, and there was considerable uncertainty about whether Jean Rhys could be called a feminist writer. Many agreed with Helen McNeil that she 'was feminine rather than feminist'.[2] Her novels might depict patriarchal oppression, but feminists as well as non-feminists felt that her heroines connived too much in their own unhappiness. Jean Rhys herself in interviews was always unwelcoming to what she suspiciously called 'Women's Lib', which she felt simplified and distorted her life, and – yet again – patronized her. At a time when appearance was of intense symbolic importance to the feminist battle, she clearly had a quite unreconstructed love of make-up and pretty clothes. But most significantly, perhaps, the kind of feminist literary theory dominant in the seventies, which concentrated on sexual oppression and rarely took account of any other, was not yet ready to take on Rhys's world where economic, racial, class, colonial and sexual oppressors all trample the disadvantaged. For all Rhys's sharp attack on the 'scorn and loathing for the female' (*VD* 20) which she saw as embedded in English culture, she is not arguing simply that all men are, as the chorus-girls put it in *Quartet*, 'swine, dearie, swine' (*Q* 14). If there is any one form of

11

oppression privileged over others in Rhys's work, it is the power of money, but even that is never seen in isolation. Her heroines feel a bond with all those marginalized or trodden down. As Frances, in 'Vienne', one of Rhys's earliest stories, says silently to the diminutive, deceived André: 'Hail, brother Doormat, in a world of Boots' (*TABL* 199).

During the eighties, feminist interest in Rhys has grown, but, even so, in the revisionary studies of women modernists which appeared during that decade (only Virginia Woolf had previously figured much in feminist studies), Jean Rhys has remained on the margins. Rachel Blau DuPlessis, who has produced the most imaginative rereadings of women modernists so far, hardly looks at Rhys's work, and Rhys scarcely features in the three-volume account of women and modernism given by Susan Gubar and Sandra Gilbert.[3] These latters' readings of women modernists are predicated on the pre-eminence of a male/female divide in the writing of the period, describing modernism (in a robustly masculinist image) as a sex war, in which naturally there can be only two sides. Rhys's work, I suspect, raises too many other issues to be accommodated in their project.[4] Rhys again makes only a fleeting appearance as a 'ghost among the expatriates' and 'outsider among outsiders' in Shari Benstock's *Women of the Left Bank* (pp. 450, 448). Benstock is conscious of the need to be aware of differences between women, though in practice she focuses mainly on difference in sexuality. Benstock has made a valuable contribution to the rereading of the work of lesbian writers of the period, but she finds Rhys unfathomably and undesirably alien. The majority of women in Benstock's study were financially very comfortable: some were rich. Nearly all came from secure social backgrounds. Jean Rhys, she points out, knew a different Paris from the other expatriates living there:

> Rhys lived outside the bounds of society, outside even the bounds of so loosely constructed and open a society as that of the Left Bank. She discovered there no island havens, no communities of writers, no women friends, who might support her talent...Instead she discovered [the Left Bank's] outer regions where streets smelled of poverty and hunger and lives were desperate and embittered. In the thirteenth *arrondissement*...Rhys spent long days of aimless walking through mean and uninteresting quarters, passed nights in cheap hotels, and made weekly visits to the Santé prison (where her

husband, Jean Lenglet, was interred for trafficking in art objects of questionable ownership). In short, she discovered a part of the Left Bank unknown to other of its residents. (pp. 448–9)[5]

By 'other residents', Benstock means the expatriates: in a striking act of Anglo-American imperialism, the entire indigenous, and indigent, population of the thirteenth *arrondissement* (an area still described by *Paris Match* as *défavorisé*) are consigned to the status of non-persons. Perhaps she has forgotten that Rhys writes ironically of Lois in *Quartet*: 'it was evident that she took Montparnasse very seriously indeed [...] she liked explaining, classifying, fitting the inhabitants (that is to say, of course, the Anglo-Saxon inhabitants) into their proper place in the scheme of things' (*Q* 48). Benstock continues:

> According to [Stella] Bowen, Rhys's fiction 'took the lid off the world that she knew, and showed us an underworld of darkness and disorder, where officialdom, the bourgeoisie and the police were the eternal enemies and the fugitive the only hero... She regarded the law as the instrument of the "haves" against the "have-nots" and was well acquainted with every rung of that long and dismal ladder by which the respectable citizen descends towards degradation.'... In Jean Rhys's fiction the Left Bank was not the setting of an exciting literary revolution in which writers enjoyed the ease of café life. Rather the Left Bank represented exhausting and degrading efforts to provide the necessities of survival...
>
> The city's margins, its peripheral limits, drew Jean Rhys like a magnet: disgusted by the sordid, she was nonetheless incapable of resisting it. (p. 449)

Drawn 'like a magnet': 'incapable of resisting' the sordid: Benstock again turns Rhys's experience of oppression, this time economic, into a choice, or more precisely, into a failure of will. She was not in the thirteenth *arrondissement* because she was poor, but because she couldn't resist the smell of degradation. In Jacqueline Rose's words, once again 'the woman becomes the horror of which she speaks'.

Benstock's disapproving tone is one not infrequently encountered in work on Rhys. The emphasis of complaint, which in the thirties had been on her immoral subject-matter, later shifted to condemnation of her and her heroines' apathy and lack of will, though, as with Benstock's censorious comment on her passive and weak-willed addiction to low life, the two were frequently fused. 'Indolence and licentiousness', according to Kenneth

Ramchand, were the traditional charges brought against the white Creoles by the English in the nineteenth and early twentieth century, the charges to which Rhys objects in Brontë, and which, in her novels, are brought against the Creoles by characters like the Rochester figure in *Wide Sargasso Sea* and Anna's Aunt Hester in *Voyage in the Dark*.[6] Writing on the white West Indians, Ramchand quotes a novel written in 1929 about the moral impairment of a young Englishman in Jamaica through two liaisons, a major one with a white Creole woman and a minor one with a coloured (curiously close to *Wide Sargasso Sea*). Its title, The *White Witch of Rosehall*, shows clearly which was the more corrupting. One of the English characters reflects,

> what a horror [these tropics] actually were. If they did not become physically the White Man's grave, they formed for him as deadly a spiritual sepulchre.[7]

White West Indian society certainly had its own kind of decadence, but indolence and licentiousness were also the two most generally ascribed moral faults to all 'native' people throughout the Empire.[8] The problem with the white West Indians was that (like Kurtz in Conrad's *Heart of Darkness*) they had gone native: they were no longer quite English, nor even, as Ramchand puts it, 'quite European'.[9] As the Rochester figure says of Antoinette, 'Long, sad, dark alien eyes. Creole of pure English descent she may be, but they are not English or European either.' (*WSS* 56) In the British tradition 'indolence' and 'licentiousness' are the qualities that mark the difference from Englishness, and even critics who pay virtually no attention to Rhys's Caribbean origin brand her with these tropes of otherness. Her sustained attack on Englishness and its proprieties continues to arouse the fear of moral contagion that association with natives always threatened: as even a generally admiring recent critic wrote, 'I suspect that in the end Jean Rhys's appeal is fairly insidious'.[10]

All in all, it is perhaps not surprising that the first critics to get away from the myths and stereotypes through which Rhys has been so often read were her fellow (though generally non-white) Caribbeans. Rather than evoking notions of a 'Rhys woman', they recognized that these fictions were exploring a troubled and divided subjectivity at a very particular historical and social nexus.[11] *Wide Sargasso Sea* appeared, by no means coincidentally, at the time when the possible existence of something called West Indian literature was first being recognized. Kenneth Ramchand in 1970, in *The West Indian Novel and Its Background*, the first full-length study of the subject, saw in *Wide Sargasso Sea* the 'alienation within alienation' and the 'terrified consciousness' (a phrase he adapted from Fanon) of the dispossessed colonizer (pp. 231, 225). The article on Jean Rhys's work which she herself liked best, and which she felt showed most understanding of her work, was one by the Trinidadian V. S. Naipaul, which appeared in the *New York Review of Books* in 1972. Naipaul was one of the first to suggest that all her writing should be understood in the light of her colonial origins:

> She was outside that tradition of imperial-expatriate writing in which the metropolitan outsider is thrown into relief against an alien background. She was an expatriate, but her journey had been the other way round, from a background of nothing to an organised world with which her heroines could never come to terms.
> This journey, this break in a life, is the essential theme of her five novels.[12]

Naipaul emphasizes her honesty and courage rather than her victimhood: he argues that it was out of her painful, deracinated existence that she had come to write fiction that was so ahead of its time: 'Out of her fidelity to her experience,' he wrote,

> and her purity as a novelist, Jean Rhys thirty or forty years ago identified many of the themes that engage us today: isolation, an absence of society or community, the sense of things falling apart, dependence, loss... What she has written about she has endured, over a long life; and what a stoic thing she makes the act of writing appear.[13]

Much of the most perceptive criticism on Rhys has continued to come from those who have focused on her as part of the tradition of Caribbean writing, who have recognized how central to her fiction are those themes identified by Naipaul, the journey, the break in a life, isolation, loss. Some of these critics make a distinction between her 'continental fiction' and her overtly Caribbean texts, concentrating on the latter, particularly, of course, *Wide Sargasso Sea*, but also *Voyage in the Dark*, in which the heroine's memories of her Caribbean childhood play so crucial a part, and the not inconsiderable number of short stories which deal with West Indian themes: some, like Naipaul, see her colonial beginnings present in all her writings.[14] But her position in that tradition has not been uncontested: the Jamaican poet Kamau Brathwaite, for example, has argued that she cannot, since neither black nor of slave origin, be considered Caribbean at all.[15] In Caribbean writing she has an ambiguous and marginal place, just as her sense of herself as a Caribbean was always ambivalent and insecure: a white Creole (if she was entirely white, something of which she was increasingly uncertain), with a Welsh father, who came to Europe at seventeen, she had memories but perhaps not roots, or perhaps only memories of rootlessness. Even as a child in Dominica she had been aware that 'the black people were more alive, more part of the place than we were' (SP 50), and she envied them for that.

Many of the early Caribbean critics were men, and were much more interested in Rhys as a West Indian than as a woman; a large omission certainly, though at that time to define her as a 'Caribbean' rather than a 'woman' writer perhaps helped them to escape the claustrophobia of reductively personal readings; to them, the political resonances of her fiction were clear.[16] The shift was clearly signalled by Wally Look Lai in what is generally credited as the first article to insist that Wide Sargasso Sea must be thought of as a West Indian novel. He wrote there: 'The encounter between Antoinette and Rochester is more than an encounter between two people: it is an encounter between two worlds'.[17] The irony of the 'personal' readings of Jean Rhys's writing has been that they deny whole areas of her personal history, seeing her as a woman with only idiosyncratic rather than cultural differences from her European equivalents.

As more nuanced feminist theories have developed, there have been some illuminating feminist approaches to Rhys. Whether or not a woman writer is consciously a feminist in late twentieth-century terms is no longer such a central issue: the question is much more how that writer as a woman has negotiated being in a world in which the feminine stands for a position of disempowerment. With the growth of interest in a psychoanalytic understanding of how femininity is formed, and of how women become locked into patterns of desire and entrapment, the exasperated question so often asked of Rhys's heroines, 'why don't they do something?' has turned into a genuinely interested enquiry. Jean

Rhys's unease at the way seventies Anglo-American feminists concentrated solely on gender has been echoed by many of her fellow-Caribbeans and by African-American women, and, as the interaction of racial, economic, gender, class, educational and national inequalities becomes increasingly apparent, Rhys's complex vision of the workings of power has gained respect.[18]

The other element of the *ad feminam* reading of Jean Rhys's work, the recurring 'Rhys woman' who is her author's mirror-image, is now also increasingly questioned. Studies of Rhys's manuscripts have shown the degree to which she wrote and rewrote her work, shifting, cutting, rephrasing, and transforming its given origins, shaping and altering the details of her personal life as she made her fiction. But more than that, confessional readings have come to feel much more problematic than they did, depending as they do on a dubious notion of willed authenticity, the simple courage to be yourself. But who are you? The perplexed uncertainty of Jean Rhys, wondering if she is her own invention ('you think: perhaps I am') is much more of our fin-de-siècle climate. The idea of the 'Rhys woman' implied that Jean Rhys was using her fiction, straightforwardly, to explain or describe the sort of person she was, rather than, as now seems the case, more problematically, to find out who someone like her could be; or to put that in another way, it implied she was creating a 'character' in the nineteenth-century sense (albeit her own character), where now it appears that she was attempting to explore a particular kind of modern consciousness. In other words again, she was read in the seventies as a realist, and is now read as a modernist. Literary critics' theories of the self have caught up with modernism.

Critics have now begun to bring these perspectives – feminist, modernist, Caribbean – together. Teresa O'Connor's *Jean Rhys: the West Indian Novels* was in 1986 the first full-length book to take into account both feminist and Caribbean issues, though, as her title indicates, it looked solely at the Caribbean novels. O'Connor does not stress Rhys's modernism, but she writes illuminatingly about literary references in her texts.[19] Since then two recent studies, one by Coral Ann Howells and one by Mary-Lou Emery, have begun to weave together all three strands in her fiction. I am sure this is the right approach, but it is not a simple project. As I suggested earlier, as a white Creole, Jean Rhys's Caribbean identity was an uneasy one. Caribbean literature is read now in terms of postcolonialism, whilst Rhys was a colonial in terms of her history, even though she can be considered a postcolonialist in her attitude to the Empire and in her employment of many postcolonial strategies. She was ill-placed to join in one major endeavour of postcolonial literature, the creation of a counter-history, a counter-identity, an alternative 'imagined community', to free the colonized from a mimicked colonial identity and from their cribbed confinement within the colonizers' history. These counter-narratives have largely been formed in masculine terms, and have raised problems for many postcolonial women writers, but additionally so for a woman in Rhys's position, who as a white West Indian was too marginal a figure to have unproblematic access to either history. Reading her as a woman writer is similarly problematic: one has to recognize that, like many other postcolonial women, her chief loyalty is not to her sex – though that does not mean that issues of gender are not crucial to her work – but to the group with which she identifies, in her case the disempowered and dispossessed, which are neither so homogeneous nor so easily identified as a group held together by race, nationality, or even class. And what does one mean by calling her a modernist? A word which embraces T. S. Eliot and Bertolt Brecht, Ezra Pound and Federico García Lorca, Gertrude Stein and Virginia Woolf is a problematic term. Certainly Rhys's poetic, elliptical prose, her concern with subjectivity and language, her irony, her themes of loneliness, anxiety and loss, her cosmopolitan, often metropolitan settings, all appear quintessentially modernist. If one wants a label, 'modernist' is certainly the most satisfactory. Yet there are some elements in her work which can be better understood in terms of her affinity with the French nineteenth-century precursors of modernism, and others which might be better described as postmodernist, not least the metafictional structure of her most famous novel, *Wide Sargasso Sea*.

So how do these multiple and divided identities come together in Jean Rhys's fiction? What is the relationship of her writing to other modernist or postmodernist texts? What has she to offer in her interpretation of European imperialism? These are the questions I shall now turn to in the rest of this essay. But before I leave this examination of the powerful myths that have so often surrounded Rhys, I want to return to Jacqueline Rose once more. she writes:

What happens if we ask, not what truth does the Plath fantasia *conceal*, but what truth does it express? Not about Plath herself in this first instance, but about the discourse of literary criticism.[20]

What truth does the Rhys fantasia express? Not about Rhys herself in the first instance, but about the discourse of literary criticism? Perhaps it is worth thinking about why the fantasy of the passive masochistic female emerged so strongly in the eighteenth century. One explanation could be that it was one way of dealing with the clash between the ideology of universal freedom espoused by Enlightenment and revolutionary thinkers, and the actual position of women. It *naturalizes* their political and cultural inferiority. One has only to read Kant's references to women to see this process at work. Analogies can be made with the tropes by which the subordinate position of the colonized was justified – their childlike incapacity, for example, or indeed their effeminacy. Such tropes hide oppression from conscious view. In the case of Rhys's work the fantasy makes it possible to blot out the darkness of her work, her depiction both of the violence and instability of the psyche, and of the cruelty which is the underbelly of Western civilisation. Rhys saw colonialism at first hand, she witnessed the growth of fascism in Europe, she experienced the harshness of a sexual code which gave no quarter to impecunious women who transgressed it. Her view of the human condition can be terrifyingly bleak. As Julia says in *After Leaving Mr Mackenzie*:

> Animals are better than we are, aren't they? They're not all the time pretending and lying and sneering, like loathsome human beings. [...] People are such beasts, such mean beasts. [...] They'll let you die for want of a decent word, and then they'll lick the feet of anybody they can get anything out of. And do you think I'm going to cringe to a lot of mean, stupid animals? If all good, respectable people had one face, I'd spit in it. I wish they all had one face so I could spit in it. (*ALM* 97–9)

And those are the words of a passive victim? Jean Rhys is, I shall argue, both a deeply disturbing social critic, who radically questions European society's values and assumptions, and a subtle and unsettling delineator of modern subjectivity.

I want now to go on to look more closely at two of her texts, one Caribbean and one continental. The Caribbean text is a short story, 'The Day They Burned the Books', in which she explores her fraught colonial inheritance: the continental text is *Good Morning, Midnight*, the fourth of her novels, set in Paris two years before the outbreak of the Second World War. These may not seem the most obvious choices, particularly as recently for some critics – and on many syllabuses and reading lists – Rhys has become the author of only one significant book, *Wide Sargasso Sea*. But whilst I believe it is true that *Wide Sargasso Sea* is Rhys's finest novel, both its literary merits and political dimension have been much more widely recognized than those of *Good Morning, Midnight*, whose equally significant political resonances have been largely ignored. *Good Morning, Midnight* will, I believe, come to be recognized as one of the great anti-fascist novels of the thirties, just as *Wide Sargasso Sea* has been acknowledged as a groundbreaking analysis of the imperialism at the heart of British culture. 'The Day They Burned the Books' is a story which is especially illuminating for an understanding of the impact of Rhys's colonial heritage on her writing. There are neglected aspects of Rhys's art which I hope my examination of these two works will open up. Finally, I shall end by looking at the evolution of her narrative technique and its relation to the themes in her work of language, memory and loss. But first, before I begin to look at my chosen examples of Rhys's fiction, I want to suggest a way of reading the autobiographical basis of her fiction which takes account of the political as well as the psychic aspects of her work.

3

Writing in the Margins

Although I have criticized those autobiographical readings of Rhys's work which identify her literally with her heroines and reduce the scope of her work to an individual plight, an autobiographical writer is of course what she is. The stories which appeared in *The Left Bank* (1927) are mainly vignettes based on her experience in Paris, a couple go back to her Dominican childhood and 'Vienne' draws on an early period in her marriage to Jean Lenglet. The source of the plot of *Quartet* (1928) is her relationship with Ford Madox Ford while Lenglet was in prison for currency irregularities. The character of George Horsfield in *After Leaving Mr Mackenzie* (1930) appears to be based on her second husband, Leslie Tilden Smith, and Julia's relationship with her sister Norah draws on Rhys's difficult relationship with her own sister Brenda. *Voyage in the Dark* (1934) is based on her affair with her first lover, Lancelot Grey Hugh Smith, and was first written as an autobiographical account some twenty-four years before it was published. The story of Sasha's marriage to Enno and the death of her baby son in *Good Morning, Midnight* (1939) draws once more on Rhys's marriage to Lenglet. Even in *Wide Sargasso Sea* (1966) many of the details are drawn from her own Caribbean childhood. The short stories that appear in *Tigers are Better Looking* (1968) and in *Sleep It Off Lady* (1976) often use incidents in her life – 'Let Them Call It Jazz', for example, has the visit to Holloway, 'Goodbye Marcus, Goodbye Rose' an experience of sexual molestation as a twelve-year-old (an experience which Coral Ann Howells argues is a crucial determinant in Rhys's psychological make-up.[1] When she came to write her autobiography, *Smile Please* (published posthumously in 1979), she was anxious to avoid repeating incidents that she had already covered in her fiction, but in the end some appear.

Anyone interested in parallels between Rhys's life and fiction can consult Carole Angier's biography, where they are extensively documented.

I don't want to deny these parallels, though they are by no means exact, rather to shift the terms in which Rhys's use of autobiography has been understood. In drawing on the events of her own life she, like others in the same period, is trying to find a narrative, a language, a form, which makes sense of the world she has experienced. Rhys distinguished between the 'truth' of her writing – to which she was committed – and the facts of her life. But to what is she being 'true'? Mellown sees it as truth to her temperament, and praises her major achievement as 'the portrayal of a psychological type never before so accurately described'.[2] I would argue that far from describing a 'type', who might have been born in riches in the nineteenth century, or in poverty in the sixteenth, yet either way would have a psychological profile similar to hers, Rhys is instead portraying a different kind of consciousness, 'never before so accurately described', a consciousness formed by the particular historical and personal circumstances of her life, yet not unique to her, rather increasingly with resonances for many others. Colonialism and its aftermath played a crucial role in the shaping of this consciousness. As Gayatri Spivak has written: 'In the figure of Antoinette, whom in *Wide Sargasso Sea* Rochester violently renames Bertha, Rhys suggests that so intimate and personal a thing as human identity might be determined by the politics of imperialism'.[3] As Catherine Belsey and Jane Moore sum up Spivak's argument here, Rhys is concerned not with 'essence' but with 'position'.[4]

Rhys's use of autobiography, I want to argue, needs to be understood as the attempt to make sense of, and to find words for, the position in which she found herself. But what was that position? One of the problems in discussing Rhys's work has been that until recently no critical language existed in which to express the ambiguity and fractured condition of identities like hers. Literary criticism and cultural analysis could happily discuss domination and oppression in terms of discrete nationalities, classes, ethnic groups. But as a Creole, Jean Rhys was culturally mixed, marginal to the metropolitan world, hybrid, always a foreigner even in her native land. She became a migrant, unsettled, on the move, with no roots to return to, no base point, a foreigner everywhere. Brought up in a bourgeois family, she found that in Europe her poverty and her transgressions of the sexual code meant she was an anomalous, suspect inhabitant of the interstices of the rigid British class system. As Neville Braybrooke commented in 1967, she wrote of those 'who belong to an in-between world ... [They] are flotsam floating between the rich and poor, just as, in the West Indies, the Creole belongs neither to white nor black.'[5]

The existence, indeed, the multiplicity of lives similar to hers, lived in ambiguity and dislocation, has become part of the general awareness only in the last few years. Cultural criticism has been transformed by a burst of intellectual creativity and energy which has brought together those two conditions of being – on the one hand, creolization, marginality, hybridity, assimilation, syncretism, and, on the other, migrancy, exile, diaspora, dispersal, travelling. In nineteenth-century Europe dislocation was predominantly the lot of farm workers moving to form the urban proletariat, a class which rarely voiced that experience: yet all the same, as Walter Benjamin so influentially argued, it was that move to the city which determined the central images and concerns of much nineteenth-century writing. But modernity has seen other forms of displacement, brought about by colonialism, by slavery, by pogroms, and now by decolonization, which have been the causes, whether ultimately or immediately, of so many movements of people in the twentieth century. Many now find themselves living what Homi Bhabha has evocatively called 'unhomely lives'.[6]

Rhys's fiction registers the sense of disorientation and the uncertain identity of those who live the ambivalent, uncentred, dislocated existences which some now argue have become paradigmatic of our postmodernist times. Stuart Hall, for example, who like Jean Rhys is from the Caribbean, commented a few years ago at a conference on *The Real Me? Postmodernism and the Question of Identity*:

> Thinking about my own sense of identity, I realise that it has always depended on the fact of being a *migrant*, on the *difference* from the rest of you ... Now, in this postmodern age, you all feel so dispersed, I become centred. What I thought of as dispersed and fragmented comes, paradoxically, to be *the* representative postmodern experience ... Welcome to migranthood ... Young black people in London today are marginalized, fragmented, unenfranchized, disadvantaged

and dispersed. And yet they look as if they own the territory. Somehow, they too, in spite of everything, are centred, in place.[7]

The result of this 'emergence at the centre of the previously peripheral and marginal' is, Iain Chambers has argued, a transformation of metropolitan culture.

The modern metropolitan figure is the migrant: she and he are the active formulators of metropolitan aesthetics and life styles, reinventing the languages and appropriating the streets of the master. This presence disturbs a previous order. Such an interruption enlarges the potential as the urban script is rewritten and an earlier social order and cultural authority is now turned inside out and dispersed. All is revealed in the dexterity of moulding the languages of modernity and cultivating the city according to different rhythms, making it move to a diverse beat. It is to speak the languages – linguistic, literary, cultural, religious, musical – of the dominator, of the master, but always with a difference. Language is appropriated, taken apart, and then put back together with a new inflection, an unexpected accent, a further twist in the tale.[8]

Chambers' evocation here of the transformations of street and popular culture by the migrant echoes the terms in which the modernist transformations of high art are usually described. The danger of this view of the new centrality of the migrant is that it can become an easy romanticism, which celebrates the creativity of street culture, but ignores the deprivation, discrimination and loneliness which are still so often the migrant's lot. Yet, all the same, it is very suggestive. If the archetypal modernist artist is, as Benjamin has it, the flâneur, the figure who chooses, indeed seeks out, marginality, who constructs an ironic difference from which to interrogate the metropolis, then the migrant, whose difference is inescapable, whose marginality the metropolis has defined but whose presence is now stubbornly transforming the metropolis, is perhaps the best choice for the representative postmodern 'formulator of metropolitan aesthetics'. There is no doubt that not only British street culture but the novel in English is being transformed by those who have come to Britain or, in Rushdie's phrase, 'write back' to Britain from what are or were Commonwealth countries.

When Rhys made her journey to England in 1907, being a migrant was for her indubitably a lonely business, very much a question of being on the edge, not the centre. Naipaul's image of 'the mysterious journey from an unknown island, the break in a life', which for him is the creative matrix of all Rhys's work, the source of her exploration of 'the themes that engage us today... isolation, an absence of society or community, the sense of things falling apart, dependence, loss', is perhaps simply an earlier, bleaker version of Hall's and Chambers' view of the migrant, on the periphery yesterday, foreshadowing the centre of today. Coral Ann Howells, trying to resolve the question of how to bring together feminist and colonial interpretations of Rhys's work, also makes her journey from the island to the metropolis the core and clue to her work:

> what Rhys constructs through her fiction is...a feminine colonial sensibility, becoming aware of itself in a modernist European context, where a sense of colonial dispossession and displacement is focused on and translated into gendered terms, so that all these conditions coalesce, transformed into her particular version of feminine pain.[9]

Howells is surely right to suggest that such a journey cannot be the same for a woman as for a man, and to emphasize the importance of the historical moment at which Rhys's journey was made, but her conclusion disturbingly reduces Rhys's work again to a woman victim's tale. Howells does not define explicitly what she means by a 'feminine colonial sensibility' but her sentence structure implies its meaning is paraphrased by the words 'a sense of colonial dispossession and displacement...translated into gendered terms', which, in Rhys's case, is 'her particular version of feminine pain'. Yet the colonial experience, for Rhys as for others, does not only bring dislocation: the position on the margins gives a perspective, a difference of view, what Iain Chambers calls the 'oblique gaze of the migrant', from which the homeland's values and institutions can be appraised and judged: it leads not just to 'pain', but to anger and resistance. Colonial dispossession in Rhys's fiction is not simply translated into sexual oppression of one kind or another. If that were so, the 'colonial sensibility' would scarcely be 'aware of itself'. Rhys's fiction takes account of a whole range of oppressions, colonial, racial, economic, sexual: being a woman does not mean that she collapses them all into the sexual, but nor does it mean that she simply adds sexual oppression at the end of the list. Being a woman means that all other oppressions are experienced in a more intense and acute form. Rhys's gender makes her more rather than less aware of her 'colonial displacement and dispossession', more rather than less aware of her critical distance from the values and conventions of the metropolis. To develop Chambers' metaphor, what Teresa de Lauretis calls the woman's 'view from elsewhere' renders her migrant's gaze yet more oblique.

Modernism, the artistic movement which she met on that journey, was in itself forging an ironic awareness and critique of those same values and conventions. As Zygmunt Bauman put it in *Modernity and Ambivalence*: 'In modernism, modernity turned its gaze upon itself and attempted to attain the clear-sightedness and self-awareness which would eventually disclose its impossibility, thus paving the way to the postmodern reassessment.'[10] Bauman offers here an illuminating way of understanding modernism's rapid evolution from its glorification of modernity and attack on nineteenth-century culture in Enlightenment terms (universality, abstraction, the privileging of the aesthetic sphere) to a sense of despair in all that the Enlightenment and modernity stood for (progress, meaning, rationality): modernism, far from being its contrary, is embryonic postmodernism. Bauman's analysis of modernism is one particularly appropriate to literature, where the impersonality, bald formalism and attempted universality of something like abstract painting or the international style in architecture was never possible. Writers cannot think of their medium in purely formal terms: language does not exist independently of history and power – the reason why, one might suggest, that the unsettling of meaning through pastiche and parody was always part of high literary modernism, though they only entered architecture with postmodernism. In Jean Rhys's case, her feminized, ex-colonial modernism radically questions the world in which she finds herself: because she writes from a position of dislocation, marginality and feminine disempowerment, she moves closer to postmodernism than some of her contemporaries.[11] This shift emerges not only in her transformations of other texts, of which *Wide Sargasso Sea* is only the best-known example, in the multiple voices in her fiction, in her fragmentary, shifting collages: even more it can be seen in her sense of the implosion of meaning, her vision of a Nietzschean void behind a coercive, cruel, imperialist and misogynist language.

4

Autobiography and Ambivalence

Bauman's rereading of modernity and postmodernity is primarily concerned with what those movements have meant for Jews marginalized and displaced by hegemonic European culture, but his work sheds light on Rhys's position and concerns. Bauman draws on Derrida's philosophical critique for his cultural analysis, arguing that modernity's drive has been to create and enforce order: ambiguity and ambivalence are anathema to it. Jean Rhys does not, of course, talk in terms of modernity or the Enlightenment, but she has a very similar view of European, particularly English society's refusal to accept difference or ambiguity. This coercive intolerance is a constant theme in her writing. In *Voyage in the Dark* Anna's stepmother Hester has

> an English lady's voice with a sharp cutting edge to it. Now I've spoken you can hear I'm a lady. I have spoken and I suppose you now realise that I'm an English gentlewoman. I have my doubts about you. Speak up and I will place you at once. Speak up, for I fear the worst. That sort of voice. (*VD* 50)

In 'Outside the Machine', a short story written probably in the fifties, set in an English clinic near Versailles, the impoverished expatriate Inez Best sees 'the fat, fair woman in the bed opposite' giving her a 'sharp sly, inquisitive' stare:

> An English person? English, what sort of English? To which of the seven divisions, sixty-nine subdivisions, and thousand-and-three subsubdivisions do you belong? [...] My world is a stable, decent world. If you withhold information, or if you confuse me by jumping from one category to another, I can be extremely disagreeable, and I am not without subtlety and inventive powers when I want to be

27

disagreeable. Don't underrate me. I have set the machine in motion and crushed many like you. Many like you ... (*TABL* 81)

The talkative chorus girl in the next bed fares better:

The fat woman opposite – her name was Mrs Wilson – listened to all this, at first suspiciously, then approvingly. Yes, this is permissible; it has its uses. Pretty English chorus girl – north country – with a happy independent disposition and bright, teasing eyes. Placed! All correct. (*TABL* 84)

The unplaceable Inez Best raises in Mrs Wilson what Bauman calls 'the horror of indetermination', the attitude which at its most extreme led to the 'identification, proscription, and extermination of those who were different'.[1] The unplaceable are 'strangers', not 'others', not, that is, recognizable, identifiable enemies; strangers are, Bauman writes,

one (perhaps the main one, the archetypal one) member of the family of *undecidables* – those baffling yet ubiquitous unities that, in Derrida's words ... 'can no longer be included within philosophical (binary) opposition, resisting and disorganising it, *without ever* constituting a third term, without ever leaving room for a solution in the form of speculative dialectics.[2]

Although Bauman is centrally concerned with the strangerhood of Jews, his argument is – and recent work on racial theory, as well as Jean Rhys herself, is on his side – that anti-Semitism was part of a continuum of prejudices which were as prevalent in England and America as in Germany. He looks particularly at the assimilated Jews, who shed their identity as Jews yet found it impossible to be accepted as part of any European nation-state: they were 'trapped in ambivalence'. For example, Kafka's life, he writes, 'is an inbetween life: in between space, in between time, in between all fixed moments and settled places that, thanks to their fixity, boast an address, a date or a proper name'.[3] Kafka, all of whose work could be called a 'voyage in the dark', was, as an assimilated Jew, neither a Gentile nor a true Jew: as a German-speaker living in Prague, not Czech, but, being Jewish, not German either. The reasons Jean Rhys found herself always a stranger were historically very different from Kafka's, but the prejudices they faced were part of the same broad process, the collapse into paranoia of European confidence in its rational order, the paranoia that Fanon describes coming about as colonialism disintegrated, the paranoia that in Europe resulted in fascism. Unlike Kafka's, Rhys's characters on the whole have names, even if those names are often changed or questioned, but, like him, Rhys writes of an inbetween world, where identities are indecipherable, uncertain, confused. In her metropolitan fictions, her characters live in transitory, anonymous boarding houses and hotels, surrounded by strangers, strangers to those who surround them. Instead of homes they can only go 'back to the hotel. To the Hotel of Arrival, the Hotel of Departure [...] Back to the Hotel Without-a-Name in the Street Without-a-Name, and the clients [with] no names, no faces.' (GMM 120) Her protagonists are always 'undecidables'. Julia, in *After Leaving Mr Mackenzie*, has had 'all the hall-marks rubbed off her' (*ALM* 12). In *Quartet*, the first question Heidler asks Marya is 'But you are English – or aren't you?'(*Q* 12). In 'Till September Petronella' Julian says, to the heroine, who has 'no money, no background and no nous', 'I can't quite make you out. [...] You ghastly cross between a barmaid and a chorus-girl.' (*TABL* 15 and 20–1) Rhys writes of women who, like the assimilated Jews, are unfailingly recognized as alien. Like Sasha's futile efforts to convince waiters that she is *une femme convenable*, their attempts at acceptance are doomed (*GMM* 82).

Bauman argues that Kafka's situation was one which paradoxically brought both impotence and insight: he quotes this passage from one of Kafka's stories:

> He has two antagonists: the first pushes him from behind, from his origin. The second blocks his road ahead. He struggles with both. Actually the first supports him in his struggle with the second, for the first wants to push him forward; and in the same way the second supports him in his struggle with the first; for the second of course forces him back. But it is only theoretically so. For it is not only the two protagonists who are there, but he himself as well, and who really knows his intentions? However that may be, he has a dream that sometime in an unguarded moment – it would require, though, a night as dark as no night has ever been – he will spring out of the fighting line and be promoted, on account of his experience of such warfare, as judge over his struggling antagonists.[4]

Bauman reads this as a parable of assimilation and its consequences, the story of

> that 'dark night' from which the hapless victim of unwinnable war could emerge as the judge of the war's futility. The victims ... could be

among the first to see through the modern dream of uniformity, the first to shake free from the modern horror of difference, the first to assault point-blank the modern religion of intolerance.[5]

Rhys's heroines are also caught in that 'unwinnable war': this is perhaps the root cause of their sense of powerlessness and paralysis. Not that they feel that way all the time: the rhythm of the novels follows their swings between resistance and defeat. If they didn't resist, it would not be a war. In Bauman's argument, it is those caught in irredeemable ambivalence, like the assimilated Jews, who are the first to see both the cruelty and the impossibility of absolutes and certainties: thrust ahead of their time, they begin 'the postmodern reassessment'. As a writer, it is to this group that Rhys belongs.

There were, of course, other modernists whose marginality was given rather than chosen. D. H. Lawrence (also patronized – in both senses of the word – by Ford Madox Ford) was always acutely aware of the difference of view his working-class beginnings gave him. James Joyce was an Irish Catholic, another ex-colonial who wrote obsessively of his origins. Both, like Rhys, were outsiders to the metropolitan establishment: both, like her, became migrants, and both, like her again, turned to their own biographies and lifeworld for the material of their fiction. For all three, the modernist interrogation of the narratives and syntax of western civilization intensified, perhaps helped to make possible, the reflexivity of their writing. As Maud Ellmann has persuasively argued, even those modernists who claimed to be most impersonal are intensely personal writers. Yet Rhys's gender distanced her even more than these male outsiders from Europe's grand narratives. Amongst the terms by which metropolitan society defined its values, those Rhys distrusted most deeply were its definitions of womanhood: 'For God knows', as Frances thinks in 'Vienne', 'if there's one hypocrisy I loathe more than another, it's the fiction of the "good" woman and the "bad" one' (*TABL* 194). And it was not only a question of the judgements of bourgeois morality. One of the particular problems modernist women faced, Rachel Blau DuPlessis suggests, was that

> In the writings of male modernists, femaleness is as fixed and eternal a category as ever before in Euro-literature...We – speaking women in historical time are faces masked with a static, unhistorical idea of Woman: a fiction, an intersection of discourses repetitive in Western

culture, whether religious, scientific, juridical.[6]

All modernist women writers had to struggle to free themselves from that mask and from that intersection of discourses; as DuPlessis says of H. D., their writing was 'the career of that struggle'.[7]

DuPlessis argues that women are what she calls '(ambiguously) nonhegemonic',

> because as a group, generally, we are outside the dominant systems of meaning, value, and power, as those saturate us, as they are 'organised and lived'. To talk of society and culture involving 'hegemonic' practices does not mean that hegemony is a ten-ton stone falling from nowhere to crush you into some shape... A hegemony, as a set of practices, has 'continually to be...resisted, limited, altered, challenged'.[8]

Even if hegemony, what Jean Rhys called in 'Vienne' 'the huge machine of law, order and respectability against one' (*LB* 241), can seem remarkably like a ten-ton stone aiming to crush the unambiguously nonhegemonic like Rhys ('I have put the machine in motion and crushed many like you...'), that hegemonic machine is what her work continually resists and challenges. Just as Rhys constantly describes her protagonists' struggles to refuse the definitions others thrust upon them, so her fiction was her attempt to reject the hegemonic view of her existence, or of existences like hers, and to find terms of her own in which to tell her story. In the clinic, Inez Best looks round her in alarm:

> [The nurses] were like parts of a machine, she thought, that was running smoothly. The women in the beds bobbed up and down and in and out. They too were parts of the machine. They had a strength, a certainty, because all their lives they had belonged to the machine and worked smoothly, in and out, just as they were told. [...] Because she was outside the machine they might come along at any time with a pair of huge iron tongs and pick her up and put her on the rubbish heap, and there she would lie and rot. 'Useless, this one,' they would say; and throw her away before she could explain, 'It isn't like you think it is, not at all. It isn't like they say it is. Wait a bit and let me explain. You must listen; it's very important.' (*TABL* 82)

Jean Rhys's fiction is her explanation, and she has something important to say.

31

Other modernist women writers besides Rhys wrote auto-biographical fiction (consider, for example, Dorothy Richardson, Djuna Barnes and Anaïs Nin) but Rhys's work can perhaps be particularly fruitfully compared with the repeated self-portraiture of the women surrealist painters of the interwar period. The version of womanhood that the male surrealists imposed on them was one which Rhys often shows enmeshing her own women protagonists, the image, as Whitney Chadwick puts it, of 'the *femme-enfant*, that volatile mix of sexual awareness and childlike ingenuousness'. As Chadwick says,

> Alienated from Surrealist theorizing about women and from the search for a magical Other, women artists turned to their own reality. Their many self-portraits reveal their rejection of the idea of woman as an abstract principle, and a substitution of the image in the mirror as a focal point in their quest for greater self-awareness and knowledge. However fantastic their imagery, it remains firmly rooted in their experience of their own bodies and in their acceptance of their psychic reality... [One woman] artist has written that 'it is surely related to myself descending into the unknown behind the mirror/looking-glass inspired by Lewis Carroll's *Alice*.[9]

Perhaps Chadwick makes it sound easier than it is. What is one's own reality? ('You think: perhaps I am?') But certainly Jean Rhys's telling and retelling of aspects of her life was both resistance and search, both an analysis of masks and a dialogue with mirrors. Like the women surrealists, she is not painting a realist portrait but descending into the unknown and uncharted, both within her inner psychic world and the inbetween world in which she lived on the margins. In her fiction those inner and outer worlds, the psychic and the cultural, are deeply intermeshed. One of the achievements of her fiction was finding a form through which their complex interrelation could be conveyed.

Homi Bhabha, in his recent analysis of 'unhomeliness', chose to look particularly at two women writers – Toni Morrison and Nadine Gordimer – because, he says, their gendered perspective deconstructs the civil state's boundary between the private and public spheres: in their work 'the unhomely moment relates the traumatic ambivalences of a personal, psychic history to the wider disjunctions of political existence'.[10] It is a description which can be extended to Rhys's fiction. Rhys's postcolonial, modernist/postmodernist fiction draws on the circumstances of her own 'unhomely' life, draws on her own experience of the 'journey, th[e] break in a life...isolation, an absence of society or community, the sense of things falling apart, dependence, loss', but in doing so she makes apparent the psychic and political consequences of 'the modern religion of intolerance', the religion which was the ideological underpinning of the colonialist project.

5

'The Day They Burned the Books'

I want now to turn to Rhys's short story 'The Day They Burned the Books', in which the anomalies and ambiguities of her colonial experience are compellingly etched. She wrote this story, in which she looks back to the Dominica of her childhood, during the years when she was working on *Wide Sargasso Sea*, though it was published six years earlier. 'The Day They Burned the Books' dramatizes the fraught racial tensions among which she grew up, and suggests how that colonial conflict influenced her evolution as a writer. The title of this island story evokes Caliban's frustrated plot to burn Prospero's books, the source of his mastery and power, and at one level this is a story about the rejection of colonialism.[1] But the story is also, and more specifically, about how the children of colonialism deal with their inheritance of love and hate, of cultural riches and cultural chains. Yet more specifically again, it is about how Rhys has become the kind of writer she is. The story is set around the turn of the century, when the colonials did not expect England's place as motherland and touchstone of civilization to be questioned, and is told by an unnamed white Creole girl, twelve at the time of the story. Like other of Rhys's stories, though written as reminiscence from an unspecified later date, it is told with the child's eye, as a cluster of vivid memories, a strategy which allows Rhys's writing imagistic immediacy as well subtle shifts and juxtapositions. The narrator's friend Eddie, small, consumptive and precocious, is the son of an Englishman, Mr Sawyer, agent for a steamship line, who has settled on the island for no apparent or determinate reason. Mr Sawyer doesn't fit in with the colonials because he isn't 'a gentleman' – drops his h's in fact. He has married a coloured woman, pretty and 'nicely educated', but he treats her insultingly and callously. His wife never complains, in public pretending it is a joke – 'this mysterious, obscure, sacred, English joke'; but the black maid Mildred says the wife's eyes have 'gone wicked, like a soucriant's eyes' (*TABL* 38). (A 'soucriant', Rhys explains in her autobiography, is a Caribbean vampire, a woman who sucks blood at night, but in the day can only be recognized by her red eyes – which in this case, as in others, could perhaps be red from weeping, *SP* 30.) Mr Sawyer has a passion for books, and builds a special room to house the piles that arrive with every mailboat. 'Once', says the narrator,

> I went there with Eddie to borrow *The Arabian Nights*. That was on a Saturday afternoon, one of those hot, still afternoons when you felt that everything had gone to sleep, even the water in the gutters. But Mrs Sawyer was not asleep. She put her head in at the door and looked at us, and I knew she hated the room and hated the books. (*TABL* 38)

Eddie, meanwhile, is being subversive in his own way. 'It was Eddie,' she says, 'who first infected me with doubts about "home" meaning England (*TABL* 38). The colonial children continually retell the tales they have heard of London's fairytale delights, which 'none of us had ever seen...the beautiful, rosy-cheeked ladies, the theatres, the fogs, the blazing coal fires in winter, the exotic food...strawberries and cream' (*TABL* 39). One day Eddie says, sacrilegiously,

> I don't like strawberries [...] and I don't like daffodils either. Dad's always going on about them. He says they lick the flowers here into a cocked hat and I bet that's a lie. (*TABL* 39)

The narrator, also 'tired of learning and reciting poems about daffodils' is shocked but delighted. The English children she has met have snubbed her:

> 'You're not English; you're a horrid colonial.' 'Well, I don't much want to be English [...] It's much more fun to be French or Spanish or something like that – and, as a matter of fact, I am a bit'. Then I was [...] [n]ot only a horrid colonial but also ridiculous. Head I win, tails you lose – that was the English. (*TABL* 39)

Eddie's father dies suddenly, and the two friends take over the room and its books;

> The blinds were always half-way down and going in out of the sun
> was like stepping into a pool of brown-green water. [...] 'My room,'
> Eddie called it. 'My books,' he would say, 'my books.' (*TABL* 40)

But one day to their horror Mrs Sawyer, accompanied by an
excited Mildred, comes to get rid of the books, good ones to be
sold, old ones to be burnt. She throws them off the shelves in fury:
'I knew bad temper (I had often seen it) I knew rage, but this was
hate.' Eddie, distraught, shrieks 'Now I've got to hate you too.
Now I hate you too' (*TABL* 41). He snatches the copy of *Kim* he
had been reading. The girl snatches a book at random, hiding it in
the front of her dress where 'it felt warm and alive'. Later, at
sunset, 'a huge, sad, frightening sunset', they sit together under
the mango tree outside the house, and Eddie cries for the first
time since his father's death, and the girl holds his hand and cries
too, and thinks, 'now we're married' (*TABL* 42–3). It's not till she
goes home that she realizes her book is 'in French and seemed
dull. *Fort Comme La Mort*, it was called...' (*TABL* 43).

She and Eddie have been expelled from their private childhood
haven by the hate colonialism breeds, precipitated into adulthood
by Mrs Sawyer's destroying rage. The conflagration is reminiscent, and yet very different, from the fire at the end of Angela
Carter's *The Magic Toyshop*, which also marks the end of
childhood, and leaves Finn and Melanie also alone, also holding
hands (pp. 199–200). Melanie and Finn may be apprehensive, but
the fire is the sign of their liberation from a coercive and tyrannical
parental world. Here, Eddie and the girl have been thrust into
premature adulthood, into the knowledge of the wounds and
malice of history, into the knowledge of the violence and
bitterness which is their heritage. Though the girl is white and
Eddie the son of a coloured woman, that distinction is less clear
towards the end of the story, which emphasizes that Eddie was
'white as a ghost', and the girl, quoting her father on the Creoles,
says, 'Who's white? Damned few' (*TABL* 42). Eddie has taken
Kipling's story of another hybrid product of colonialism: his copy
has even lost its first twenty pages so Kim's unquestionably white
origins have gone. The children hate the arrogance of the English,
but they want access to European culture, though not necessarily
in the form the colonial power would give it to them. Mrs
Sawyer's rebellion against her past oppression is magnificent:

She was breathing free and easy and her hands had got the rhythm of tearing and pitching. She looked beautiful, too – beautiful as the sky outside which was a very dark blue, or the mango tree, long sprays of brown and gold. (*TABL* 41)

'Decolonisation never takes place unnoticed', wrote Fanon, 'for it changes individuals and modifies them fundamentally. It transforms spectators crushed with their inessentiality into privileged actors.'[2] The colonials had approved of Mrs Sawyer for being such a decent, respectable, submissive coloured, looking so 'nice' at the funeral, weeping the right amount at the right moment, though her meekness had not earlier made easier the ambivalent position of the Sawyer household, his class and her colour, which is hinted at by a reference to their having 'once *ventured* [my italics] to give a dinner party' (*TABL* 39). Jean Rhys said of this story: 'It is about the West Indies a good while ago when the colour bar was more or less rigid. More or less' (JRL, 105). When Mrs Sawyer's silent hatred erupts into violence, what pours out is hatred not only of her husband but of the culture that has made him what he is. Hate is Mrs Sawyer's right, the story shows, yet her hate is still, as hate must be, cruel, destructive and terrifying. And there is another dimension to the husband, which the colonial children do not understand: a man who drops his h's but has a passion for books would have been an object of ridicule back in England: he too has been oppressed by Englishness. The children were on Mrs Sawyer's side. They love her beauty, inseparable from the beauty of the island. But they are on the side of the books too. Mrs Sawyer had been caught between races: 'you damned, long-eyed, gloomy half-caste', as Mr Sawyer used to call her. The children are caught between cultures. Mr Sawyer had been caught between classes. No one is judged in this story – except perhaps the snobbish English children – and nobody is happy.

'The Day They Burned the Books' is about both external and internal margins, and margins, as Mary Douglas argues in *Purity and Danger*, her influential study of the concepts of pollution and taboos, are always areas of dangerous ambivalence. Seen from England, the colonials are outside the boundaries of the homeland; seen from Dominica, with its 300 whites in a population of 30,000 (CA, 5), they are outsiders to the non-white majority, both to the coloured Mrs Sawyer and the black maid Mildred, who band together against the external authority of the colonial legacy.

The Sawyers are caught in anomalous interstices: Mrs Sawyer, a coloured, is neither part of the white nor the black community; Mr Sawyer, educated but lower-class, is a déclassé. But then, in terms of empire, the colonials too are on an internal margin, an ambiguous group between the imperial metropolis and the colonized. 'The horrid colonials' are despised by the British and hated by those of slave descent. In her autobiography, *Smile Please*, Jean Rhys talks about the first time she realized she was hated because she was white, describing the experience in language strikingly reminiscent of 'The Day They Burned the Books'. She was sent to a mixed convent school (her father being unusually liberal), and early on sat next to a very pretty coloured girl; she admired her and 'long[ed] to be friendly', so, she writes,

> I tried, shyly at first, then more boldly, to talk to my beautiful neighbour.
> Finally, without speaking, she turned and looked at me. I knew irritation, bad temper, the 'Oh, go away' look; this was different. This was hatred – impersonal, implacable hatred. I recognised it at once and if you think that a child cannot recognise hatred and remember it for life you are most damnably mistaken. [...]
> They hate us. We are hated.
> Not possible.
> Yes it is possible and it is so. (*SP* 49)

Her description of this experience, along with her account, a couple of chapters earlier, of how her black nurse Meta ('the terror of my life') hated to see her read, suggests something of the way in which her fiction grows out of her life – by no means straightforwardly, but as a means of working out and thinking through what the events in her life have meant. She writes that Meta 'always seemed to be brooding over some terrible, unforgettable wrong' (*SP* 29). In Mrs Sawyer's story she finds a local habitation and a name for such a sense of wrong. The historical legacy of slavery must enter every Caribbean life in a different way, and in the Sawyers' marriage Rhys creates one particular 'unhomely moment' which can, in Homi Bhabha's phrase, 'relat[e] the traumatic ambivalences of a personal, psychic history to the wider disjunctions of political existence'.

For the children too in this story, the traumas of a 'personal, psychic history' are inseparable from the political. 'The wider disjunctions of political existence' take meaning in the individual's psyche. For Eddie, the tragedy of colonialism is foremost his personal Oedipal tragedy: no longer with the hope of assuming the place of the hated father – only his father's sneer, 'clamped to his face', is left – he has now also 'got to hate' his mother, of whom he says, as a kind of love-elegy, before he starts to cry:

> She's prettier than your mother. When she's asleep her mouth smiles and she has your curling eyelashes and quantities and quantities and *quantities* of hair. (*TABL* 42)

Has he a way forward? The story ends without telling us. At the beginning of the story we have been told 'people said that he... wasn't long for this world' (*TABL* 37). What about the girl? The story contains two hints. The first, perhaps, is more an omen than a hint: as Mrs Sawyer throws down the books, the girl sees that Christina Rossetti's poems, though in leather like Byron and Milton, are to be burnt, not sold:

> by a flicker in Mrs Sawyer's eyes I knew that worse than men who wrote books were women who wrote books – infinitely worse. Men could be mercifully shot; women must be tortured. (*TABL* 41)

In the context it is a chilling evocation of the vocabulary of violent revolution, but it tells the reader where the young girl will go, even though it will be a painful passage. If there is hatred around, it will be fiercer for women. The other hint comes in the reference to Maupassant's novel, *Fort comme la mort*.[3]

6

Fort Comme La Mort: the French Connection

Jean Rhys had some anxieties over whether the significance of this reference would be understood: she wrote to Selma Vaz Dias in 1953, when she sent her an early version of this story:

> I don't think I've got over what I meant when I called the book 'Fort comme la mort' – However it could be done if you like it. I don't suppose you will for most people find it dull. I like it of course because it's about what used to be my home. I've never had another anyway. (JRL, 105)

Fort comme la mort is unusual in Maupassant's oeuvre in having as its subject an artist working in Paris. Rhys's experience of France, where she lived for most of the twenties and first began writing for publication, and of French writers, in particular the pre-modernists like Flaubert, Maupassant and Rimbaud, played a vital and emancipatory role in her development. According to Carole Angier she began each of her first four novels in Paris. France and French writers were of crucial importance to early Anglo-Saxon modernism, particularly on the eve of the First World War, but Rhys's response to French artistic culture was particularly long-lasting and intense. By the end of twenties, Pound was more interested in Confucius and Eliot in Christianity. Many of the expatriates living in Paris in the twenties and thirties had little contact with the French or (and here Ford was certainly an exception) interest in French writers. Rhys had a very different view of her years in France from Shari Benstock's dire picture of her outcast wanderings: she had no regrets about being an 'outsider among outsiders' in the expatriate community. Even if she was in the thirteenth *arrondissement* because she couldn't afford the Faubourg St Germain, she preferred the Parisian half-world to that of the expatriates. In 1964, she wrote to Diana Athill about a book she had read on Paris in the twenties by someone 'not an Englishman':

> He stresses something no one here realises at all. The 'Paris' all these people write about, Henry Miller, even Hemingway etc was not 'Paris' at all – it was 'America in Paris' or 'England in Paris'. The real Paris has nothing to do with that lot – As soon as the tourists came the *real* Montparnos packed up and left. Here is an extract. [...] 'These so called artists with dollars and pounds sterling at the back of them all the time! As immoral as they dare...and when they return to their own countries it's always on the back of Paris they put everything they have done. Considering no Parisians will have anything to do with them...'
> That is quite true. And if I saw something of the other Paris – it's only left me with a great longing which I'll never satisfy again. (JRL, 280)

It was in the 'other' Paris, more than anywhere else, that she met people with whom she could feel an affinity: but, in addition, France provided her with the nearest to a cultural home she ever found, the nearest to a literary mother-tongue. Jean Rhys's route out of her cultural impasse was by identifying herself as an artist with an alternative cultural tradition to that of the imperial centre. In postcolonial writing that is not an unusual strategy, but the circumstances are generally quite different. The colonized reassert their own traditions in the place of those imposed on them by the colonizers: for example, the Nigerian Chinua Achebe's early work, or the Caribbean Edward Brathwaite, who went back to the African roots of black Caribbean culture, and advocated the use of 'nation-language' rather than 'Standard' English. In Rhys's in-between position, searching for origins was not an option: her homeland traditions were already alien in one way or another. She had to look for a more oblique strategy. The one she found had much in common with Samuel Beckett's solution to his not dissimilar position: Beckett, as an Anglo-Irish Protestant, was also a kind of Creole – neither part of the Home Country nor wholly native to his native land. (When Beckett was asked in Paris if he were English, he famously replied, *'Au contraire'*.) In aligning themselves with the French, the *bête-noires* of English conservatism, each opened up a position from which they could write. Rhys did not, of course, go as far as Beckett in actually writing in the French language, though French often appears in her texts, but a comparable distancing was at work. Although – to her regret – she was never to settle in Paris in such a permanent way as Beckett did, she wrote to Francis Wyndham in 1964 about her years on the continent: 'for a long time, for years, I escaped from an exclusively Anglo Saxon influence and have never returned to it' (JRL, 281).

It is possible Frenchness did for Rhys represent some kind of fragmentary and oblique association with a homeland tradition. Dominica had been a French colony until 1805: the black Dominicans spoke French patois, and were Catholics. Though like most of the colonials there Rhys was a Protestant, under the influence of her convent school she longed to become a Catholic and, having been given extra French lessons, began to love French poetry. She was not bilingual, but her early knowledge of the language stood her in good stead: her French became excellent, and she at one stage helped to support herself and her first husband by translating French novels and stories. Martinique, Dominica's sister island and still French, often carries particular symbolic significance in her fiction – Antoinette's mother and Christophine in *Wide Sargasso Sea* are from Martinique, and references to Martinique figure resonantly in *Good Morning, Midnight*. In some ways there seem to be parallels between her attitude to blackness and Frenchness, or at least to the world of the French demi-monde: just as a child she had longed to be black, so as an adult she longed to be in Paris. The expatriates' sense of superiority to the native French may have played a part in endearing the latter to her: Rhys is on the side of anything despised by the Anglo-Saxon bourgeois, and bourgeois she is very sure these expatriates are, with their 'dollars and pounds sterling at the back of them', and only 'as immoral as they dare'. This is, after all, one of the themes of *Quartet*.

However that may be, at first sight Rhys's enthusiasm for the French might seem surprising, when her dislike of the English was so tied up with their arrogant imperialism, of which the French were certainly also guilty. She was well aware that the French could be quite as oppressive and as hypocritical as the English. In *Quartet*, when Miss De Solla says that the English 'touch life with their gloves on. They're pretending about something all the time', Marya thinks to herself, 'Everybody pretends [...] French people pretend every bit as much, only about different things and not so obviously' (*Q* 9). The proprietor of Marya's hotel, Madame Hautchamp, who looks 'like a well coiffured eagle with a gift for bargaining' is the epitome of respectable coercion:

> Madame Hautchamp was formidable. One heard the wheels of society clanking as she spoke. No mixing. [...] All so inevitable that one could only bow the head and submit. (*Q* 31)

Her husband is quite as chauvinist as any Englishman depicted in Rhys's fiction. He deeply suspects 'the strange young couples who filled [his wife's] hotel – internationalists who invariably got into trouble sooner or later'. Told of the Polish Stefan Zolli's arrest, he returns to his newspaper

> with an expression of profound disapproval [...] continu[ing] his article, which, as it happened, began thus:
> *Le mélange des races est à la base de l'évolution humaine vers le type parfait.'*
> 'I don't think,' thought Monsieur Hautchamp – or something to that effect. (*Q* 27)

In the diary she kept while her third husband was in prison (very much the same time as she was beginning work on 'The Day They Burned the Books'), Rhys tried to understand why she hated the English and loved France:

> Always like a constant aching, no, an irritation, harsh, gritty, this feeling about England and the English. [...] It was Jack, who is a writer, who told me that my hatred of England was thwarted love. I said disappointed love maybe.
> I swear that looking out of the porthole that early morning in Southampton, looking at the dirty grey water, I knew for one instant all that would happen to me. [...]
> I never once thought this is beautiful, this is grand, this is what I hoped for, longed for. [...]
> Then why did I feel it in Paris? (*SP* 165, 168-9)

It is a passage, incidentally, which once again illustrates the complexity of the relation between her life and her fiction – the disillusionment with Englishness which becomes part of the pattern of 'The Day They Burned the Books' was something she only experienced once she reached England. In that story she has found an image that can carry a whole range of the elements that

went to make 'the break in [her] life'. But perhaps part of the
answer to her question about Paris – which she doesn't answer
there – is that the French tradition she aligned herself with was a
dissident one in France itself, on the side, as she saw it in *Boule de
Suif*, of the prostitutes against the 'meannesses and cant and spite'
of the bourgeoisie. In an early review, D. B. Wyndham-Lewis
wrote of her work: 'The form of Miss Rhys's studies is purely
French... They are French in their poise, directness, and clarity'.[1]
It is true her style was influenced by French models, though not
only by the qualities identified in this very Anglo-Saxon view of
French writing – equally important was what she learnt from
Maupassant about how to write about madness or from Rimbaud
about the use of fantastic imagery.[2] But it is not only for her a
question of style, but also of a French tradition of anti-bourgeois,
anti-establishment alignment of the writer with those despised by
respectable society, almost an 1890s, Yellow Bookish admiration
of the demi-monde.

The affinity the modernist Rhys has with both the 1890s and the
postmodern can again be traced to her position on the margins of
European culture. Metropolitan periodization does not necessarily apply to those outside the centres of power, as Paul Gilroy has
argued in *Black Atlantic*, which deals with another marginalized,
anomalous group, black intellectuals. Gilroy puts forward what
one might call a creolized, diasporic interpretation of contemporary Black American–European culture, rejecting any search for
essential or authentic origins. Like Bauman in his discussion of
the Jews, Gilroy is dealing with a history in itself quite different
from Rhys's life-world, yet his naming of this discontinuous,
many stranded, transnational culture the 'Black Atlantic' in itself
compares strikingly with Rhys's title for her deepest exploration
of the colonial experience, *Wide Sargasso Sea*. The 'wide Sargasso
Sea', so famous for its flotsam, perhaps stands simultaneously for
the vast expanse between the two worlds of her life, and for the
never-completed journey between them, the turbulent, unstable
existence of those in-between cultures.[3] Gilroy evokes the image
of a ship as a chronotope or representative image with which to
understand this composite history: Rhys too used the boat as an
image for her life, certainly not becalmed, but not necessarily
getting anywhere either.[4] She wrote to Francis Wyndham:

Now I'm Le Bateau Ivre as well as the Volga boatman but always a boat for some reason and in stormy weather too [...] no stormy isn't the word. More like one wave after another knocking against the rocks [...] Do you know 'Oh mon Dieu/La mer est si grande/Ma barque est si petite'? (JRL, 276–7)

The part of Gilroy's work, however, that I want to relate particularly to Rhys are his comments on the nature of Black Atlantic time, what he calls a 'syncopated temporality' in which, as Ralph Ellison put it, 'Sometimes you're ahead and sometimes behind'.[5] Gilroy draws on Toni Morrison's suggestion that 'modern life begins with slavery' and that 'black women had to deal with post-modern problems in the nineteenth-century and earlier... certain kinds of dissolution, the loss of and the need to reconstruct certain kinds of stability'.[6] But if, as he suggests, the temporality of the margins is not necessarily that of the metropolis, syncopated temporality, sometimes ahead and sometimes behind can also apply to the colonies, especially to the slave-owning Caribbean. Modern life was born with the discovery of the New World, with the exploitation of its wealth, its inhabitants and the African slaves who laboured there. The cruelty and oppression on which the wealth of the modern Europe was based were seen most starkly there. As Jean Rhys wrote, 'There is an atmosphere of pain and violence about the West Indies. Perhaps it wasn't astonishing that I was tuned into it.'[7] After emancipation, the economy of the Caribbean collapsed. In one sense the white Creoles were by the mid-nineteenth century already living in the aftermath of modernity. But in another way, colonies are always behind, and the hierarchies of class and colour more obviously and rigidly preserved. Hence perhaps Rhys's affinity for those French nineteenth-century assaults on the uncompromising bourgeoisie, and hence too perhaps, when she went to Europe, her ability to have simultaneously a postmodern sense of the meaninglessness of English snobbery and a nineteenth-century insight into its vicious efficacy.

7

The Politics of
Good Morning, Midnight

In Maupassant's story, what is *fort comme la mort*, strong as death, is love.[1] In Rhys's story, it is hate. The memory of being hated and rejected as a child and the impossible desire to be accepted as a friend by the Dominican blacks always remained with Rhys, fictionalized most powerfully in the relationship between Antoinette and Tia in *Wide Sargasso Sea*.[2] Yet hatred and its power to damage and maim are also central themes in Rhys's continental novels: in those as well, hate is the outcome of a politics of oppression, demarcation and fear.

Helen Tiffin, writing on Jean Rhys, suggests that 'the white Creole is, as a double outsider, condemned to self-consciousness, a sense of inescapable difference and even deformity in the two societies by whose judgements she always condemns herself'.[3] Such internalization of rejection and hostility, she points out, is charted by Rhys in both her Caribbean and her continental fiction. *Good Morning, Midnight* is a city story, not an island story, a story of the metropolitan centre rather than the colonial periphery, a story of the beginnings of middle-age rather than the end of childhood. Yet its account of how subjectivity is formed and deformed through exclusion, prejudice, marginality and hatred has ultimately much in common with 'The Day They Burned the Books'.

Sasha Jensen, the narrator and central character of *Good Morning, Midnight*, is part of society's flotsam, an outsider, impecunious, a woman of fading looks and uncertain reputation, condemned, like the Creole, to self-consciousness of difference and deformity by the judgements of those around her:

> Those voices like uniforms – tinny, meaningless.... Those voices they brandish like weapons [...] Qu'est-ce qu'elle fout ici, la vieille? What the

devil (translating it politely) is she doing here, that old woman? What is she doing here, the stranger, the alien, the old one? . . . I quite agree too, quite. I have seen that in people's eyes all my life. I am asking myself all the time what the devil I am doing here. All the time. (*GMM* 46)

Sasha has lived in London for five years, where she has 'two-pound-ten a week and a room [. . .] off the Gray's Inn Road'. The present time of the novel covers part of a brief visit she makes to Paris, where she has an abortive encounter with a gigolo called René, and a fleeting friendship with a painter called Serge. Much of the novel is taken up with her memories of the past, particularly of her earlier life in Paris, of her experience then of a sometimes loving, occasionally hopeful, often painful marriage, of her baby's death and the final departure of her husband. But although Sasha knows Paris well, the only person she sees whose name she remembers is a café-owner of whom she is terrified (he may think she has aged), whose looks she cannot interpret: '[Theodore] smiles, his pig-eyes twinkle. I can't make out whether his smile is malicious (that goes for me too) or apologetic (he meant well), or only professional'(*GMM* 43). When she uses the word 'familiar' it is of a café lavabo, not of a home, nor a face. It is mirrors, not people, who are 'well-known'. Not that she is the only outsider: the city is full of nameless strangers, whose origins can only be guessed at, who may be cruel, may be kind, may be dangerous, may be sad. As Rachel Bowlby has pointed out, in this novel national labels, all identities, are uncertain and insecure.[4] When Sasha meets the gigolo – well, she assumes he's a gigolo – he claims to be French-Canadian: she thinks he's Spanish or Spanish American, while the patronne of her hotel thought him English. He claims to have run away from the Foreign Legion in Morocco through 'Franco Spain' (*GMM* 63): Franco's army came from Morocco. Perhaps he was fighting for Franco. Perhaps not. Sasha is wearing a fur coat, still left from a more affluent past: he thinks, or she thinks he thinks, that she is rich. She meets two men in the street, tries to guess their nationality under a lamp-post: Germans? Scandinavians? They claim to be Russian, though one has a French name. They ('tactfully') don't even try to guess hers. Sasha is, presumably, English, her former husband Enno presumably Dutch, but the reader can never be sure. Yet, for all the unreliability of the labels, the city can tell who are acceptable, who are not. Derrida's 'undecidables', Bauman's 'inbetween identities', are instantly recognized and execrated. In Rhys's fiction, even inanimate objects threaten 'the stranger, the alien' with Dickensian menace:

> Walking in the night with the dark houses over you, like monsters. If you have money and friends, houses are just houses with steps and a front-door – friendly houses where the door opens and somebody meets you, smiling. If you are quite secure and your roots are well struck in, they know. They stand back respectfully, waiting for the poor devil without any friends and without any money. Then they step forward, the waiting houses, to frown and crush. No hospitable doors, no lit windows, just frowning darkness. Frowning and leering and sneering, the houses, one after another. Tall cubes of darkness, with two lit eyes at the top to sneer. (GMM 28)

Kenneth Ramchand praised Rhys's Caribbean stories for their evocation of 'the brutality of this [colonial] world, with its busy gossip, its whisperings and its sanctimoniousness...its envy, malice and hatred'.[5] A similar atmosphere pervades this novel – and, to a lesser extent, her other continental fiction – though in the European context critics have often seen this sense of menace as a symptom of her (or the Rhys woman's) personal paranoia.[6] The colonial-bred Rhys's 'terrified consciousness' must certainly have sensitized her to the violence and fear behind European respectability, but the paranoia she evokes is not just, in Mellown's term, that of 'a psychological type', but of an epoch. She is describing the febrile nightmarish world of Europe on the eve of the Second War World, with its anti-Semitism, its racism, its class-machinery, its nationalistic posturing. Rhys's writing demonstrates in fictional form Robert Young's terrifying proposition that the Holocaust was not an aberration: 'Fascism was simply colonialism brought home'.[7] She recognizes, with her 'oblique gaze of the migrant' that the 'modern religion of intolerance' is at work in both.

In 'The Day They Burned the Books', Rhys shows both the hatred of the oppressed for their oppressors, and the hatred felt by the hegemonic for the different. It is with the latter that Good Morning, Midnight is primarily concerned. In Purity and Danger, when Mary Douglas looks at those two currents in social groups, she distinguishes between 'powers' and 'dangers': on the one hand the power of those in authority, the power which claims legitimacy, on the other a nebulous, indeterminate dangerousness attributed to the interstitial, to the ambiguous, to those who do not fit in. Douglas gives as an example of such feared marginal figures Jews in English society, where 'belief in their sinister but indefinable advantages in commerce justifies discrimination against them – whereas their real offence is always to have been outside the formal structure of Christendom'.[8] Witchcraft, she says, is ascribed to those in the 'inarticulate, unstructured areas' of society: witches are

> social equivalents of beetles and spiders who live in the cracks of the walls and wainscoting. They attract the fears and dislikes which other ambiguities and contradictions attract in other thought structures, and the kind of powers attributed to them symbolise their ambiguous, inarticulate status.[9]

The analogy between the fear and dislike of the ambiguous and fear and dislike of insects is one which Rhys also evokes – in the Caribbean, the poor whites in *Wide Sargasso Sea* are jeered at as 'white cockroaches': in the Home Counties, the unplaceable Petronella in 'Till September Petronella' is called a 'female spider'. Douglas's analysis is a generalized account of the kind of process which Bauman (who quotes Douglas) has identified in the project of modernity, the fear and rejection of the inbetweens, which reached its most extreme moment in the Holocaust. In fact, one might ask whether the reason Douglas's analysis has been so widely influential is that, whether or not it is true of other cultures, she has seized on something that helps to explain modern western culture to itself. Certainly both kinds of power or supposed power identified by Douglas, established authority and marginal threat, and the anxiety and hatred which they each excite, appear in Rhys's fiction, in none more acutely than in the eve of war world of *Good Morning, Midnight*. For Rhys, established authority is not simply the institutionalized power of the state, but racial, economic and class privilege as they are used by individuals to oppress or coerce others – in some ways what we might think of as a quite Foucauldian view of the diffusion of power.[10] Rhys is almost invariably on the side of those oppressed by so called legitimate power or social propriety: as Ford so rightly said, she has 'a bias of admiration...and of sympathy' for criminals and prostitutes. She accepts the inevitability of the hatred that her beautiful coloured schoolmate or Mrs Sawyer have for the whites, even though she shows the psychic devastation it inflicts. What she passionately exposes and excoriates is the hatred which the domineering, the xenophobic or the simply respectable have for the different and the unplaceable. But in either case, hating or being hated remain destructive processes in her work.

Good Morning, Midnight is set, unusually precisely for Rhys, in October 1937. Rhys was then, like Sasha, living in London, but she too spent a short holiday in Paris, in November 1937, beginning the novel on that visit, and finishing it about a year later. The great International Exhibition which took place in Paris in 1937, and which Rhys herself visited, is mentioned at the beginning and the end of the book. Those references, Mary-Lou Emery has suggested, situate the novel 'within a Paris of intense social and political conflict, symbolized best perhaps by the two major buildings of the exposition which confronted one another directly on each side of the Champs de Mars – that of the Soviet Union, topped by giant figures of a marching man and woman with hammer and sickle held high, and that of Nazi Germany, crowned by an immense gold eagle grasping a swastika in its claws'.[11] In 1937 France was divided and unstable. The Fascist leagues, whose violent demonstrations – Virginia Woolf described them as a fascist revolution – brought down the government in 1934, were officially disbanded by the reforms brought in by Léon Blum, but were still thoroughly active. Blum, a Socialist and France's first Jewish premier, had put in place a range of humanitarian economic legislation, but had been forced to resign that June, opposed by right and left. The French were uneasily aware of the Fascist pressures on their borders. Franco was by then in charge of all of northern Spain, well on his way to victory; Hitler had occupied the Rhineland in 1936: Mussolini was pursuing his imperialist ambitions in Abyssinia. In the England Sasha has left, Mosley's British Union of Fascists, in spite of legislation against them, had attracted alarming support in the London County Council elections and were still holding their anti-Semitic marches. The Duke and Duchess of Windsor were, that very October, paying an admiring visit to Hitler. In the year Rhys spent writing this novel, the threat of war steadily grew. To read Rhys's continental fiction as divorced from this political context is as mistaken as it would be to ignore the impact of colonialism in her Caribbean stories.

Rhys's sense of the political forces at work in European society has much in common with the analysis Virginia Woolf made in her 1938 essay *Three Guineas*. Woolf and Rhys, of course, inhabited and wrote of very different areas of the social map: indeed, as several critics have noted, Sasha's 'two-pound-ten a week and a room just off the Gray's Inn Road', is an ironic reference to Woolf's *A Room of One's Own*.[12] Certainly 'a room' means very different things to each of them. For Woolf a room of one's own is privacy within the bourgeois home: for Rhys a room is never home, only the latest bleak retreat from a hostile world. If Woolf is the modernist flâneuse, who after her street-haunting returns to a welcoming domesticity, the postmodernist migrant can only go back to her temporary and friendless lodging, indistinguishable from the last, 'always the same room [...] the damned room grinning at me. The clock ticking. Qu'est-ce qu'elle fout ici, la vieille?' (*GMM* 120, 150). But though their experience of the social system may be very different, there is much about it on which they agree. In *Three Guineas* Woolf argues that patriarchy, racism, pomposity, militarism, economic exploitation, autocracy, and fascism are all part of the same process. For Woolf, fascism was the apotheosis of patriarchy: addressing men, she writes,

> You are feeling in your own persons what your mothers felt when they were shut out, when they were shut up, because they were women. Now you are being shut out, you are being shut up, because you are Jews, because you are democrats, because of race, because of religion... The whole iniquity of dictatorship, whether in Oxford or Cambridge, in Whitehall or Downing Street, against Jews or against women, in England or Germany, in Italy or Spain is now apparent to you.[13]

Jean Rhys was perhaps less hopeful than Woolf that Establishment Englishmen would find such connections 'now apparent', and it has to be said that *Three Guineas* had a chilly reception from Woolf's usual male sympathizers. Yet this pattern of oppressions, and the power of what Rhys calls 'organized society' (*ALM* 17) to enforce them is shown at work in all her writing. Woolf's ambivalent relationship with left-wing politics is becoming increasingly well-documented. Not much research has yet been done on Rhys's political attitudes, but what evidence is available suggests that, even if she had no links with any political organizations, she too leant ambivalently to the left. As a young girl, her support of the blacks earned her the family name of

'Socialist Gwen', though 'socialist' in that context, of course, had no more terminological exactitude than 'commie bastard' in Reaganite America. Her first husband, who influenced her deeply, and whom she had seen again shortly before her visit in 1937 to Paris, had attended the Congress of Writers Against Fascism in 1936, and reported the Spanish Civil War for the *Daily Herald*.[14] In the Second World War both he and their daughter Maryvonne were to work for the Dutch Resistance. For some months before the Spanish Civil War, Rhys and her second husband had living with them a young writer called Esmond Romilly, a relation of Winston Churchill, who had run away from Wellington School and his highly respectable family.[15] They gave him a home until he joined the International Brigade, later marrying his fiercely radical cousin Jessica Mitford. Rhys was very fond of Esmond, and appears to have been in sympathy with his views. She was certainly, her letters show, appalled by Franco's actions, and by the right-wing English press reaction to them (JRL, 31). In those prewar years, she made a friendship that was to last several decades with a left-wing white Dominican, Phyllis Shand Allfrey, who eventually went back to be Dominica's Minister of Labour. Serge Rubin, the Russian Jewish painter in *Good Morning, Midnight*, who is presented as the single most admirable male figure in Rhys's continental fiction, is a man 'of the Extreme Left' (*GMM* 86)[16] But Rhys was certainly not of the left in any simple or dogmatic way. Rhys's views, judging from her fiction, probably have much in common with the maverick, sexually libertarian, feminist, anarchic individualism of Dora Marsden's *The New Freewoman* and *The Egoist*, a philosophy which was shared, briefly at any rate, by the imagists and other early modernists. Perhaps another example of syncopated time. In spite of their leftish sympathies, Woolf and Rhys both, it seems clear, were as uncertain about the absolutes of political creeds as about any other absolutes.[17] But that does not mean that they had no politics, rather that there was no contemporary formulation that took in their range of concerns, sexual, racial and (particularly for Rhys) economic exploitation, nor that recognized, in Woolf's words, that 'the public and the private worlds are inseparably connected...the tyrannies and servilities of the one are the tyrannies and servilities of the other'.[18]

8

The Huge Machine of Law, Order and Respectability

Three Guineas is concerned with those within the bourgeois bastions of patriarchal society. Rhys deals with its outcasts. Woolf writes about those 'daughters of educated men' who have remained 'shut up' in the patriarchal home, Rhys about the daughters of educated men who have gone to the bad. Sasha has 'extremely respectable' relations, Marya comes from 'presentable people', but they have slipped into a social limbo, reached all the more rapidly because they have always lacked money. What their alternative might have been is vividly illustrated in *After Leaving Mr Mackenzie*, by Julia's 'good' sister Norah, who looks after her sick mother in a second-floor flat in Acton, and is

> labelled for all to see. [...] 'Middle class, no money'. [...] Everything about her betrayed the woman who has been brought up to certain tastes, then left without the money to gratify them; trained to certain opinions which forbid her even the relief of rebellion against her lot; yet holding desperately to both her tastes and her opinions. [...]
>
> Everyone always said to her: 'You're wonderful, Norah, you're wonderful. I don't know how you do it.' It was a sort of drug, that universal, that unvarying admiration – the feeling that one was doing what one ought to do, the approval of God and man. It made you feel protected and safe, as if something very powerful were fighting on your side. (*ALM* 53, 75)

'The huge machine of law, order and respectability', to use the phrase from 'Vienne', may be on Norah's side, but it is crushing her just as effectively as if she were, like Julia, defying it. 'Beasts and devils', Norah thinks, just for a minute, before sinking back into despairing conformity. Norah is one of the women whom Rhys shows policing the borders of respectable society, but she makes it clear, as so often, that police are themselves recruited from an oppressed class.

Good Morning, Midnight deals with those who have something very powerful fighting, not on their side, but against them: 'organized society' whether expressed as economic exploitation, anti-Semitism, racism or sexual prejudice. Yet like other anti-fascist artists of the period – I am thinking particularly of Brecht and Grosz – Rhys expresses her outrage through satire as well as sadness. Sasha's telling of her tale is intensely moving, but it is also very funny. She presents herself much of the time as a figure of clown-like ineptitude, while the figures of authority are ludicrous grotesques. Sasha repeatedly finds herself bullied by self-important bourgeois men, like the scowling patron of her hotel, 'a fish, lording it in his own particular tank, staring at the world outside with a glassy and unbelieving eye' (*GMM* 13). She remembers being sacked as a Parisian shop assistant by the English manager, 'the real English type', whom she refers to by the Kafkaesque name of Mr Blank. (Even in this Paris-based novel the true acmes of autocracy are English):

> ...He arrives. Bowler-hat, majestic trousers, oh-my-God expression, ha-ha eyes – I know him at once. [...]
>
> He looks at me with distaste. Plat du jour – boiled eyes, served cold ...
>
> Well, let's argue this out, Mr Blank. You, who represent Society, have the right to pay me four hundred francs a month. That's my market value, for I am an inefficient member of society, slow in the uptake, uncertain, slightly damaged in the fray, there's no denying it. So you have the right to pay me four hundred francs a month, to lodge me in a small, dark room, to clothe me shabbily, to harass me with worry and monotony and unsatisfied longings till you get me to the point when I blush at a look, cry at a word. We can't all be happy, we can't all be rich – and it would be much less fun if we were. Isn't that so, Mr Blank? There must be the dark background to show up bright colours. Some must cry so that the others may be able to laugh the more heartily. Sacrifices are necessary . . . Let's say that you have this mystical right to cut my legs off. But the right to ridicule me afterwards because I am a cripple – no, that I think you haven't got. And that's the right you hold most dearly, isn't it? You must be able to despise the people you exploit [...] Did I say all this? Of course I didn't. (*GMM* 17, 25-6)

Mr Blank is, like Sir William Bradshaw in *Mrs Dalloway*, the representative of patriarchy in its entrenched dehumanizing authority, cold, efficient, scornful. For Rhys, as for Woolf, this self-righteous, brutal authority pervades the social system. In the notebook she kept while writing *Good Morning, Midnight*, Rhys shows it at work again, evoked by the same imagery, this time at the level of the state. Commenting on British foreign policy (presumably in the context of the Munich crisis) she wrote of:

> This dear country of ours which has attained its present envied position by the simple expedient of betraying all its friends one after the other and always for strictly moral reasons... You've got to do it with a straight face and honest eyes too. 'Honest eyes our speciality – Plat du jour – Boiled eyes served cold'.[1]

Rhys has a complex view of the relations between gender and power: she certainly never uses such abstract – one might say patriarchal – language as 'patriarchy'. Since for her, as I have argued, the power structures of organized society depend on a complex interaction of economic, class, racial, national and gender privilege, if there is a faultline in society it runs not between men and women as such, but between the haves and have-nots, the secure and the unacceptable – though in her fiction, far more men are among the haves, far more women among the have-nots, and many of her characters, male and female, are, like the white Creole woman, both oppressed and oppressing. Teresa O'Connor argues convincingly that for Rhys the colonized Caribbean is woman-identified and imperial England male-identified, and in many ways and instances that is true: the cold logic of the metropolis against warm sensuality of the islands, the Englishmen who 'don't give a damn about women', 'don't really like women' (*VD* 70 and *Q* 92) against the beautiful, passionate women, like Antoinette and Mrs Sawyer, who are identified with the islands. The Caribbean men who are domineeringly or cruelly masculinist are, whatever their colour, associated with Englishness – those who make use of an authoritarian Christianity like Godfrey or Daniel Cosway in *Wide Sargasso Sea*, or the black policeman in 'Temps Perdi', whose callousness is such, the narrator says, that 'it might have been an Englishman talking' (*TP* 159). For Rhys, patriarchy – and I think one can argue a concept of patriarchy, if not the word, is present in her work – is the power assumed and wielded by males who are, like the fish-eyed *patron*, the élite of their particular tank – whether that tank be the government, business, family or shabby hotel. In much of Rhys's fiction, patriarchy's workings appear most ruthlessly in the bourgeois double standard and its fusion of sexual and monetary values. Well-to-do men can make use of poor women as they please: a poor woman, once she is soiled goods, is an outcast. The double standard imprisons respectable women as much as it exiles the others, but it can only work with their cooperation. Without those like Norah, who rejects her scandalous sister, or Lois, prisoner of her belief in Heidler as 'the man, the male, the important person, the only person who matters', the system would break down. The rigid social demarcations laid down by Hester in *Voyage in the Dark* and by Mrs Wilson in 'Outside the Machine' continue, in their bourgeois enclaves, the pattern analysed by Leonora Davidoff in her compelling study of the way certain women in nineteenth-century England controlled entry into 'the best circles'.[2] Men who lack money, have the wrong accent, belong to the wrong race, are excluded too.

What Rhys struggles against most fiercely in the face of this hegemonic authority is what she was later to call 'thought control' (JRL, 100). What Sasha fears most about Mr Blank is not simply that he has the economic power to make use of, or alternatively dispense, with her labour. Even more damaging is that he wants to control her self-definition, he wants her to accept that he has the right to nominate her ridiculous and despicable. The seizing of definitions of morality and worth by the representatives of the coercive power of organized society is what appals Rhys. Even if the women Rhys describes are not 'shut up', as Virginia Woolf puts it, in the sense of being confined to the home, they are frequently shut up in the sense of being silenced. Did Sasha say all this to Mr Blank? She did not. The novel as a whole can be read as Sasha's attempt to give her version of her story: events and spoken dialogue are interwoven with her inner commentary, the speeches she wishes she had made, the connections she inwardly makes, the memories which return. Like Inez Best, she wants to insist, before she is thrown on the rubbish heap, 'It isn't like you think it is, not at all. It isn't like they say it is [. . .] let me explain' (*TABL* 82). As Sasha says (inwardly) to the man who won't give his girl shoes or Sasha herself any food, 'If you're determined to get people on the cheap, you shouldn't be surprised when they pitch you their own little story of misery sometimes'(*GMM* 75).

'Talking back', as critics like Nancy Harrison and Coral Ann Howells have commented, occurs throughout Rhys's fiction, even though it often takes the form, as here, of a response which is thought rather than uttered. Rhys's narrative technique, Harrison points out, turns what is silence in terms of plot into inner speech, constructing a dialogue between the powerful (who speak out loud) and the disempowered (who speak inwardly).[3] In addition, Sasha's own narrative is often split, creating a wholly internal dialogue within a psyche torn between contradictory emotions. Sometimes she shifts from first to second person: 'For God's sake, I think, pull yourself together' (*GMM* 18). Most dramatically, at the end of the novel, the shift is between first and third, as Sasha listens to 'her voice in my head', a voice which is the internalized contempt with which she lacerates herself. Sometimes even inanimate objects like the room or a looking-glass speak to her: the lavabo mirror at the Deux Magots tells her, 'I keep a ghost to throw back at each one' (*GMM* 142); the room asks 'Quite like old times [...] Yes? No?' (*GMM* 90). She imagines other people's silent comments: 'a strange client, l'étrangère' (*GMM* 59). And, repeatedly, voices from the past echo in her head. What the text of *Good Morning, Midnight* inscribes through its interweaving of these outer and inner, past and present voices is Sasha's continual, embattled attempt to make sense of her life, her struggle to resist, defy, redefine hegemonic definitions. Forging a counter-discourse, which is how Rhys's postcolonial critics describe this process, is never an easy task. The text follows Sasha's swings from defiance to defeat, from apathy to anger: she is uncertain, unsure, outraged by the so-called morality which judges her, but never confident of her power to hold it at bay. At times she feels the safest answer is to 'fly, fly, run from those atrocious voices, those abominable eyes' (*GMM* 22). If she is not as ridiculous and despicable as Mr Blank would have her believe – and much of the time she fears he is right – what is she, and, as she asks herself 'all the time' (*GMM* 46), what is she 'doing here'?

9

Resisting the Machine

Early in the novel we are introduced to Sasha's strategies for keeping her sense of disintegration and worthlessness at bay. She organizes her life as a series of rituals; designed, like the rituals of long-term prisoners, to hold on to some control over her own being ('a place to eat at midday, a place to eat at night, a place to have my drink...I have arranged my little life'); designed to evade hostility, fear, the destructive definitions of other people:

> My life, which seems so simple and monotonous, is really a complicated affair of cafés where they like me and cafés where they don't, streets that are friendly, streets that aren't, rooms where I might be happy, rooms where I never shall be, looking-glasses I look nice in, looking-glasses I don't, dresses that will be lucky, dresses that won't, and so on. (*GMM* 40)

She plans ways to ensure that 'Tomorrow I'll be pretty again, tomorrow I'll be happy again, tomorrow, tomorrow...' (*GMM* 48). She constantly re-invents herself: a new hair-dye, a new hat, another visit to the lavabo mirror to cover up tears with powder, to construct a new face, to make herself up, in both senses of the phrase. All Rhys's protagonists are creative artists: creating themselves is their only steady occupation. Even so, they can never rival the 'charming, malicious' dolls Sasha saw in the fashion house: 'What a success they would have made of their lives if they had been women. Satin skin, silk hair, velvet eyes, sawdust heart – all complete' (*GMM* 16).

Looking-glasses (both 'looking-glasses I look nice in, looking-glasses I don't') are a leitmotiv in Rhys's work, perhaps for much the same reasons as they were in the paintings of the women surrealists. Her protagonists spend a good deal of time looking in mirrors, sometimes at photos, even at ghosts of themselves, descending into the unknown, searching for some understanding of their being which is other than the definitions thrust upon them. Tiffin suggests that, for the white Creole, the impossibility of identifying either with the English or with the black Caribbeans is what makes so imperative the search in the looking-glass for an alternative image.[1] Though Rhys's protagonists recognize, some-times painfully, that the image is not identical with the self, these mirrors offer some partial anchor. For Rhys, as for Lacan, whose essay on the mirror-image was first published in 1937, the year in which *Good Morning, Midnight* is set, the image in the mirror is a misrecognition, yet even so essential in enabling the emergence of an 'I'.[2] Naming and mirroring are intimately connected in Rhys's fiction: when, near the end of *Wide Sargasso Sea*, after Antoinette's husband renames her 'Bertha', she sees 'Antoinette drifting out of the window with her scents, her pretty clothes and her looking-glass':

> There is no looking-glass here and I don't know what I am like now. I remember watching myself brush my hair and how my eyes looked back at me. The girl I saw was myself yet not quite myself. Long ago when I was a child and very lonely I tried to kiss her. But the glass was between us – hard and cold and misted over with my breath. Now they have taken every thing away. What am I doing in this place and who am I? (*WSS* 147)

The looking-glass in Rhys's fiction does not provide an escape from the rift between the self that defines and the self defined, between the self that invents and the invented self.[3] But it offers the chance to trace a tentative, approximate identity.

If Rhys's sense of the divided, precarious nature of identity is perhaps what makes her so conscious of the coercion of those who would thrust their own definitions on the disempowered, it also allows her to show another, politically resonant, form of mirroring in her texts. This is the process by which her protagonists recognize themselves, or something like themselves, in others. After Coulibri has been set on fire by the blacks, Antoinette wants, instead of leaving with her white family, to run back to her black childhood friend Tia:

> We had eaten the same food, slept side by side, bathed in the same river. As I ran, I thought, I will live with Tia and I will be like her [...] When I was close I saw the jagged stone in her hand but I did not see

her throw it. I did not feel it either, only something wet, running down my face. I looked at her and I saw her face crumple up as she began to cry. We stared at each other, blood on my face, tears on hers. It was as if I saw myself. Like in a looking-glass. (*WSS* 38)

'As if I saw myself': like the face in the looking-glass the image she sees is herself, yet not quite herself; the politics of imperialism have both made them alike and separated them for ever. Joyce has a phrase in *Ulysses* which seems particularly apt, 'aliorelative identification'; in other words, I take him to mean, seeing oneself reflected, even though not exactly, in another's experience.[4] This process is found throughout Rhys's writing. It is present, for example, in 'The Day They Burned the Books', where the girl-narrator comes to recognize, in what happens to Eddie, her own cultural 'alienation within alienation' and the pain of the cleavage between childhood and adulthood, which in this colonial context brings loss both of mother and motherland. It shapes the form of an early story like 'La Grosse Fifi', where the young Roseau sees her own vulnerabilities and loss in the ageing prostitute Fifi: it underlies the late stories in which Rhys writes about those destroyed by colonial Caribbean society, like Mr Rammage and Jimmy Longa. It is a strategy which evades the tyranny of the rigid assertions of Self and Other on which imperialism depends: it transvalues inbetween identities. 'Aliorelative identification' in Rhys's fiction is both a psychic process, the finding of a provisional, partial identity by which better to understand the turmoil of consciousness that makes up the self, and a political illumination, a new insight into her protagonists' relation to the power structures of society.

What Rhys shows in these recognitions is similarity, not of 'character', but of 'position'. Seeing how organized society treats others who are not acceptable, others living in the margins, her protagonists have more understanding of their own lives: they can recognize in them the emotional storms, despair, anger, hope, compassion, hate and need, which their position brings. In *Good Morning, Midnight* Sasha is enabled, through seeing herself mirrored in others, even though imprecisely, to find a different way of looking at her place in the world from the one Mr Blank offers her. She can judge Mr Blank with the oblique gaze of the migrant, rather than be fixed by his 'boiled', 'abominable' eyes.

There is a range of these partial, provisional, 'aliorelative identifications' in *Good Morning, Midnight*. Some are quite fleeting – the ageing woman whom Sasha sees desperately trying on hat after hat, her face

> hungry, despairing, hopeful, quite crazy. At any moment you expect her to start laughing the laugh of the mad. [...] Watching her, am I watching myself as I shall become? [...] But she is better than the other one, the smug, white, fat, black-haired one who is offering the hats with a calm, mocking expression. [...] If I must end like one or the other, may I end like the hag. (*GMM* 57–8)

Sasha sees contrasting aspects of herself in two of the Russians she meets as fellow aliens in Paris. (Sasha's Russian name, which, in another re-invention of herself, she adopted in preference to Sophia, might suggest a symbolic bond.)[5] She comes across three Russians in all on her visit, but she has nothing in common with the first – an optimist, too reasonable, 'one of those people with bright blue eyes, and what they call a firm tread' (*GMM* 47). She sees no more of him. About the second, Delmar, she has mixed feelings. He is melancholy, as she often is, and has a philosophy of life which in certain moods she finds deeply tempting:

> You didn't ask to be born, you didn't make the world as it is, you didn't make yourself as you are. Why torment yourself? Why not take life just as it comes? You have the right to: you are not one of the guilty ones. [...] When you aren't rich or strong or powerful, you are not a guilty one. (*GMM* 55)

As she listens, Sasha is half convinced, yet she remains deeply ambivalent towards him:

> I don't know why I don't quite like him [...] Perhaps it is because he seems more the echo of a thing than the thing itself. One moment I feel this, and another I like him very much, as if he were the brother I never had. (*GMM* 56)

Delmar offers disengagement, non-intervention, evil as a far-away country of which we know little: very thirties solutions, which chime with Sasha's desire – at times – to escape desire:

> Saved, rescued and with my place to hide in – what more did I want? I crept in and hid. The lid of the coffin shut down with a bang. Now I no longer wish to be loved, beautiful, happy or successful. I want one thing and one thing only – to be left alone. (*GMM* 5)

To be the echo of a thing rather than the thing itself. But neither desire nor guilt can be so easily killed. 'As soon as you have reached this heaven of indifference you are pulled out again' (*GMM* 76). That is what she is thinking when she meets the third Russian, the Jewish painter Serge.

Sasha is wary of Serge to begin with: he has 'that mocking look of the Jew, the look that can be so hateful, that can be so attractive, that can be so sad' (*GMM* 76). But he is not mocking her. Like Sasha, Serge is conscious of the prejudice about him, and angry at the cruelty that it inflicts. Gradually he 'starts getting hold of' her (*GMM* 78). He plays her Martinique music, a song about 'Pain of love / Pain of youth': they find they share a love of 'negro music', which for Rhys represents the world of the emotions ('life according to my gospel' (JRL, 45) as opposed to the hard-boiled, calculating world of the English.[6]

Although in this novel Sasha is not apparently in any literal sense a Creole, the Caribbean imagery which links Sasha and Serge suggests a side of her painfully alive both to suffering and desire, unlike the side which, like Delmar, longs for numbed disengagement. Here, at the centre point of the novel, Sasha, the stranger, the alien, listens to the exiled Jew tell the story of a mulatto Martiniquaise he met in London, living with a man not her husband, unable to go out because she cannot stand the hatred in English eyes. Serge, although he had had 'a fine suit...looked quite an Englishman from the neck down', didn't 'much like the way they looked at him either...[they had] cruel eyes' (*GMM* 79). He saw the Martiniquan woman, drunk and crying, asking for more drink, after a child called her 'a dirty woman' and said 'I hate you and I wish you were dead'. Sasha, too, is called a dirty woman, a 'sale femme', 'sale vache'. 'Why didn't you drown yourself in the Seine? We consider you as dead' her family have said to her (*GMM* 36). She too responds by getting drunk, crying, asking for more drink. In the symbolically and politically linked experience of these three, Rhys suggests the common workings of fascism, racism and bourgeois patriarchy, the persecutory power of the modern religion of intolerance. One feminist critic has expressed surprise that the Martiniquan woman's story is retold by a man, but that is perhaps to miss the point of Serge's Jewishness.[7] Like a diaspora of the dispossessed, this novel evokes a communality of the excluded. As Homi Bhabha has said of Toni Morrison:

To live in the unhomely world, to find its ambivalencies and ambiguities enacted in the house of fiction, or its sundering and splitting performed in the work of art, is also to affirm a profound desire for social solidarity: 'I am looking for the join...I want to join ...I want to join.'[8]

The people described in *Good Morning, Midnight* are casualties of the European world of 1937: people of the margins, of the ambiguous shadow land at society's edge. As Rhys was to write at the beginning of *Wide Sargasso Sea*, 'They say when trouble comes close ranks. [...] But we were not in their ranks' (*WSS* 15). The same is happening in troubled prewar Europe; ranks are closing through fear; the marginal are ever more aggressively marginalized. Rhys's protagonists search for an escape from their isolation, from their unhomeliness: they look for love, for acceptance, for a chance to join. As she leaves, Serge gives her hand a 'long hard shake' ('The touch of the human hand...I'd forgotten what it was like, the touch of the human hand') and says 'Amis'. Sasha, for a moment, feels 'very happy' (*GMM* 84). But if Rhys's fiction enacts moments of joining – like Eddie and the girl under the mango tree, like Serge and Sasha as they shake hands – these moments rarely last, and often what has joined them in those moments is only the shared recognition of pain or loss.

Serge was based on the Russian Jewish painter Simon Segal, whom Jean Rhys met on her 1937 visit to Paris. In his *Self-Portrait*, which is reproduced in Carole Angier's biography, he has given himself an exaggeratedly Jewish nose: it is the portrait of a man profoundly conscious of his difference and of society's condemnation of his difference ('I didn't much like the way they looked at me either', as Serge puts it). Rhys's linking of his response to anti-Semitism with her own experience of European xenophobia and bourgeois sexual taboos is perhaps another example of the way in which she transmutes the material of her life into the pattern of her books. In *Good Morning, Midnight*, Sasha, the impoverished Jewish painter, the woman from Martinique, are all unwelcome in metropolitan European society: they mutually reflect their shared condition as rejects, pariahs. On that same visit to Serge, Sasha buys a picture of another outsider, who in some ways represents all three of them, a painting of an old Jew, with a red nose, playing a banjo, the instrument traditionally used by black musicians. (Rhys had bought a picture, *Old Man with Banjo*, from

Segal: whether in the original the old man was a Jew, and if so, how one could tell – another exaggerated nose? – isn't clear, but in the novel the Jewishness again has important symbolic resonances.) For Sasha, the old man evokes all her life. 'He is singing "It has been", singing, "It will be"' (*GMM* 91).

> He'll stare back at me, gentle, humble, resigned, mocking, a little mad. Standing in the gutter, playing his banjo. And I'll look back at him because I shan't be able to help it, remembering about being young, and about being made love to and making love, about pain and dancing and not being afraid of death, about all the music I've ever loved, and every time I've been happy. I'll look back at him and I'll say: 'I know the words to the tune you're playing. I know the words to every tune you've ever played on your bloody banjo. ' (*GMM* 155)

Segal wrote to Rhys shortly after she returned to England, describing the old man as 'misérable, digne et résigné comme le sont les sages, les artistes et les fous. Peut-être vous donnera-t-il du courage' (JRL, 137). Rhys has drawn on those words, but she has again transformed them to give shape to her own meanings. She has fused them, for one thing, with a poem by Dorothy Parker, a woman whose skill in the mordant tragicomic has much in common with Rhys's own: 'Well and bitterly I know/All the songs were ever sung/All the words were ever said'.[9] This old Jew with his red nose (a clown? an alcoholic? merely the unloveliness of age?) sings songs which, like the Martinique music, recall the pain of love, pain of youth – its happiness too, but happiness now remembered for its loss.

Serge has other paintings of society's failures and down-and-outs, but he does not only paint pictures: he also makes masks, which to Sasha look like the pompous, condemnatory, inquisitorial figures which haunt her mind. She picks up a mask whose 'close-set eyeholes which stare into [hers]' evoke all those other 'glassy eyes', 'piggy eyes', 'boiled eyes', 'lit eyes', 'abominable eyes' which have tried to fix her in the course of the novel, and which culminate in her surreal fantasy of a world that has shrunk to an enormous machine with white steel arms with an eye at the end of each. If the old Jew is a reminder of human sadness, the masks suggest human cruelty:

> I know that face very well: I've seen lots like it complete with legs and body.

That's the way they look when they are saying: 'Why don't you drown yourself in the Seine?' That's the way they look when they are saying: 'Qu'est-ce qu'elle fout ici, la vieille?' That's the way they look when they are saying: 'What's this story?' Peering at you. Who are you, anyway? Who's your father and have you got any money, and if not, why not? Are you one of us? Will you think what you're told to think and say what you ought to say? Are you red, white or blue – jelly, suet pudding or ersatz caviare? (*GMM* 77)

This is Sasha's other great form of resistance, perhaps her most powerful strategy for resisting defeat by the machine: mockery, satire and self-irony. To return to Mr Blank: Sasha was there not simply recording her oppression but satirizing the bombastic self-importance of his kind, mocking their platitudinous cruelty. At the same time she mocks herself for the risible terror into which she is cast by this repellent, stupid man. What Sasha says she fears most is 'sink[ing] to the accompaniment of loud laughter', or, in Wilde's words, which the novel quotes, 'the laughter, the horrible laughter of the world – a thing more tragic than all the tears the world has ever shed' (*GMM* 115). Yet Sasha's narrative is in control of the laughter and mockery in her story: she, not Mr Blank, decides who is ridiculous. I spoke earlier of Rhys's writing as a search for a counter-discourse. In all her writing there is, in Voloshinov's words, a struggle for the sign, a contest between organized society's version of events, the huge machine's definitions of morality and the ones which Rhys offers. Yet, while Rhys is relentless in her deconstruction and mockery of the codes of power, her alternatives, like her protagonists', are provisional, tentative, conflictual and uncertain. So, before I go on to make some final comments on this struggle for meanings in her work, I want first to look at the moments when she shows Sasha's strategies for resistance fail.

10

The Enemy Within

What undermines Sasha's struggle to avoid the hostile gaze of others, her self-invention, her search for acceptance, even her mockery, is her own self-doubt. Like the Creole, she has internalized the condemnation and scorn of those around her. Rhys's psychic patterning of those excluded and humiliated is something far more complex than the pathos of oppression. Hatred breeds hatred, brutality breeds brutality. If Delmar reflects Sasha in her attempts to shut out the world through withdrawal and apathy, and Serge her emotional vulnerability and moments of compassion and warmth, there are other drives within her. I talked earlier of the lure of the fantasy of the willing victim; it is a lure which all Rhys's protagonists at times feel, the temptation to escape the fight against denigration by embracing and eroticizing abasement. Yet Sasha, in her relation with the gigolo, is in no sense a victim; indeed, she attempts to be a victimizer. She is conscious that René is another of her quasi alter egos – he trades on his sexuality as she has so often traded on hers – but for most of her relationship with him she plans to inflict on him the pain and humiliation that others have made her feel. Significantly, the passage in *Good Morning, Midnight* most often quoted to show the 'Rhys woman's' masochism suggests in its context more tangled, ambiguous motivations, for it occurs while Sasha is rejecting the gigolo's plea to go to bed with him, is trying, in fact, to be hard and ruthless, to avenge her own earlier suffering at the hands of men on him. A sudden fantasy sweeps across her mind like a scene remembered from a film:

> I am in a whitewashed room. The sun is hot outside. A man is standing with his back to me, whistling that tune and cleaning his shoes. I am wearing a black dress, very short, and heel-less slippers. My legs are bare. I am watching for the expression on the man's face

66

when he turns round. Now he ill-treats me, now he betrays me. He often brings home other women and I have to wait on them, and I don't like that. But as long as he is alive and near me I am not unhappy. If he were to die I should kill myself. (*GMM* 147)

It is a deeply disturbing picture of humiliation accepted, of total dependency. On one level this fantasy is an expressionist redramatization of an earlier memory in the story of a moment of intense inner emotional struggle with her husband Enno. He has insulted her brutally, gone off for three days, leaving her almost penniless, returns and immediately orders her to peel an orange: 'Now' she thinks

is the time to say 'Peel it yourself', now is the time to say 'Go to hell', now is the time to say 'I won't be treated like this'. But much too strong – the room, the street, the thing in myself, oh, much too strong ... I peel the orange, put it on a plate and give it to him. (*GMM* 108)

They make love. Is love possible without humiliation for an impoverished woman? Humiliation and how to cope with it, in the fearful, feverish world of Europe in 1937, is a theme explored in this text on many levels – sexual, racial, economic. If this fantasy is emotionally reminiscent of Sasha's bruised defeat in her relationship with Enno, the woman in the scene is not only Sasha herself. The way she is dressed suggests a girl Sasha saw earlier, washing dishes in a bar-tabac: 'Bare, sturdy legs, felt slippers, black dress [...] I know her. This is the girl who does all the dirty work and gets paid very little for it. Salut!' (*GMM* 87). Watching her, Sasha realizes, appalled, that in spite of her sympathy and identification (another dirty woman), she herself is one of the girl's oppressors. Like the white Creole with her guilty heritage from slave-owners, in 1937 the daughters of educated men, however come down in the world, are still with some of the advantages of an oppressing class. Sasha struggles to keep her guilt at bay, trying to distance the girl again:

And don't her strong hands sing the Marseillaise? And when the revolution comes, won't those be the hands to be kissed? Well, so Monsieur Rimbaud says, doesn't he? I hope he's right. I wonder though. [...] The hands that sing the Marseillaise, the world that could be so different – what's all that to me? What can I do about it? Nothing. I don't deceive myself. (*GMM* 88–9)

The girl's incorporation in the later fantasy suggests, perhaps,

67

that, unlike Delmar, Sasha cannot ultimately believe that she is a 'guiltless one'. Rimbaud, whose fervent revolutionary poem she refers to here, had written of hands 'whose flesh sings Marseillaises and never prays for mercy'.[1] Monsieur Rimbaud was not right: the oppressed are frequently forced to pray for mercy. But they may also rebel – in that Rhys agrees with Rimbaud – or at any rate imagine the possibility. Sasha has other fantasies. She sees that vignette of humiliation when she attempts to seize control, but when earlier she is desperately trying to hide her humiliation after being (she fears) ridiculed in a café, she fantasizes brutal revenge as she meekly leaves:

> Never mind ... One day, quite suddenly, when you're not expecting it, I'll take a hammer from the folds of my dark cloak and crack your little skull like an egg-shell. Crack it will go, the egg-shell; out they will stream, the blood, the brains. One day, one day ... One day the fierce wolf that walks by my side will spring on you and rip your abominable guts out. Now, now, gently, quietly, quietly.... (*GMM* 45)

One way of talking about these psychic extremities would be to call them sadomasochistic impulses. Sadomasochism, one could argue, is the psychic landscape of fascism, where fantasies of mastering or surrendering to mastery are turned into political reality, the ultimate outcome of the tyrannies and servilities of which Woolf wrote.[2] The strength and courage of Rhys's analysis is that she understands that the psyche of those victimized is the mirror image of the victimizer. She shows a fragmented, volatile, destructive psyche born of a torn, destructive, violent history. Sasha was not the only one saying in 1937, 'Human beings are cruel – horribly cruel'. It shouldn't be forgotten that this novel is set in a Paris whose intellectual élite were from 1933 to 1939 listening enthralled to Alexander Kojève, whose 'terrorist conception of history', as Vincent Descombes puts it, made violence, sacrifice and the struggle between Master and Slave the defining facts of human progress.[3]

Yet sadomasochism is perhaps an inadequate term for Sasha's swings between anger and self-abasement, her bitter struggle against the sense of worthlessness and defilement thrust upon her and her frequent defeat by it. Like Marya, who identifies with the homeless cats in the Paris streets, one of the most painful, most self-immolating identifications Sasha makes is with a sexually diseased kitten with 'an inferiority complex and persecution mania and nostalgie de la boue and all the rest', whose

> terrible eyes [...] knew her fate. She was very thin, scraggy and hunted [...] all the male cats in the neighbourhood were on to her like one o'clock. She got a sore on her neck and the sore on her neck grew worse.
> 'Disgusting' said the [...] English wife. 'She ought to be put away'. (GMM 47)

This fated, sickening cat had come to Sasha's room for safety: she

> crouched against the wall, staring at me with those terrible eyes and with that big sore on the back of her neck. She wouldn't eat, she snarled at caresses. She just crouched in the corner of the room, staring at me. (GMM 47)

In the end Sasha can't stand it, chases her off, 'still staring at me' and the cat runs straight under a taxi. When Sasha looks in the mirror, after her feared ridicule in the café, her eyes are like that kitten's eyes. It's an identification filled both with self-loathing and with guilt. When Sasha says all human beings are cruel she is not excepting herself: that is why it is such a searing truth.

Julia Kristeva has given an account of such psychic turbulence which strikingly evokes the disintegration and inner revulsion that Rhys portrays in Sasha's dark moments. Earlier I mentioned Mary Douglas's anthropological analysis of the symbolic meaning of margins, polluted, taboo, yet paradoxically full of dangerous power: in *Powers of Horror*, Kristeva draws on Douglas's work to offer a psychoanalytic reading of this process of fearful, fascinated exclusion, which she calls abjection. For Kristeva the abject, while neither the Other nor an Other, is something not quite the ego, but 'the inbetweeen, the composite, the ambiguous', the borders of the ego, that which marks it off from what it is not.[4] The abject, she argues, is formed as the first beginnings of separation from the mother, that rejection which makes the subject possible. So the abject both threatens and validates subjecthood, it both entices and repels; abjection is on the borderline between cognition and feeling, between the conscious and unconscious, 'a composite of judgment and affect, of condemnation and yearning, of signs and drives'.[5] For Kristeva, psyches which have never successfully made that separation from the mother, who have broken away violently and clumsily, who have never really taken on the Law of the Father – she gives the examples of phobics, obsessionals, borderline cases between neurosis and psychosis – are most threatened by the abject: anything inbetween, whether physically inbetween, like vomit, slime, blood, or socially, like Jews, homosexuals, sexually aberrant women, menaces their frail yet rigid egos. This fear of the abject, she says, is present in us all; we all have egos whose brittle defences can easily crumble. All religions have had cathartic rites to deal with the abject, whether defined as pollution, defilement or the sacred. In the modern secular world, where the weakening of the social/symbolic order intensifies the dread of the abject, that cathartic role, she suggests, is taken on by art.

Kristeva discusses a range of writers whose work has this cathartic power, but she looks in most detail at the frenzied, ecstatic paranoia found in both the literary works and political pamphlets of the anti-Semite and Nazi Louis Céline. Céline is Rhys's counter-image – xenophobic rather than the feared foreigner, disgusted by female sexuality rather than the despised sexual female – but for that very reason Kristeva's analysis is illuminating in reading Rhys. Kristeva quotes a passage from an anti-Semitic pamphlet Céline wrote, also in 1937 (*Barricades pour les Massacres*), which sounds as if it could be a description of the insecurely labelled aliens of *Good Morning, Midnight*:

> The Jews, you know, they're all camouflaged, disguised, chameleon-like, they change names like they cross frontiers, now they pass themselves off for Bretons, Auvergnats, Corsicans, now for Turandots, Durandards, Cassoulets . . . anything at all . . . that throws people off, that sounds deceptive.[6]

Rhys's protagonists are those whose subjectivity has been assaulted and maimed by the projection of others' fears of abjection on to them, and by their internalization of this terror. This is, perhaps, another way of expressing what Tiffin called the 'inescapable sense of difference and even deformity' of the white Creole, of the mulatto, of the Jew, of the migrant. If the anti-Semite rails against the 'undecidables' because he fears that their lack of identity threatens his, what about society's undecidables themselves? They can have no certain identity because they are identified as the unplaceables. They stir up the fear of abjection, because the unplaceable is what 'disturbs identity, system, order.

What does not respect borders, positions, rules.'[7] At times Sasha can simply mock the Mr Blanks who keep the system in order, who abhor and fear her placelessness, but when she talks of streaming blood and brains she herself has been sucked into the fantasies and psychic horrors of abjection.

For Kristeva, following the conventional psychoanalytic quest for private and familial origins, abjection goes back to the first break in a life, the first loss, the separation from the 'maternal entity', which, throughout life, we desire and fear, which represents warmth, darkness, oneness, joining, before self-consciousness, before order, before systemization, before labels, before language. But surely such psychic fracturing can be caused or exacerbated by other kinds of 'violent, clumsy' breaks in life, by, for example, the multiple losses, disorientations and inner splittings of the migrant.[8] The elements which Naipaul saw as central to Rhys's writing, the break in a life, isolation, the sense of things falling apart, dependence, loss, are perhaps both the causes and symptoms of the migrant's fragile identity and sense of abjection. If it is self-loathing that undermines Sasha's resistance, it is her experience of loss which has left her so vulnerable. The sense of loss permeates Rhys's writing, as many critics have noted. For Sue Roe, who has written particularly movingly on the sense of loss in Rhys's fiction, it is most strikingly the loss of lovers; for Deborah Kelly Kloepfer its essence is the loss of the mother; for Mary-Lou Emery, the loss of place. Perhaps prioritizing one kind of loss over the other is not to the point: all those losses are there in Rhys's writing, echoing and intensifying each other. The rift with the mother is often inseparable from the rift with home and country, as it is in 'The Day They Burned the Books', where Mrs Sawyer is both mother and the island: the abandonment by lovers often seems a repetition of those earlier rifts.[9] The most poignant loss in *Good Morning, Midnight* is Sasha's loss of her son, born in an absurd, unhomely world, in a 'place for poor people' – 'No Jesus, no mother, no chloroform either' (*GMM* 50). He is too delicate to survive without money for proper care, another victim of the 'huge machine'. 'The thought that they will crush him because we have not money – that is torture' (*GMM* 50).

What is so disturbing about the death of Sasha's son is how clean it is, how light, how quiet, how orderly, how separate; the closeness, mingling, embodiedness, messiness of motherhood is hardly there. Sasha fears her baby is too white, too pale, too silent. She has no milk. She and he are each bound in bandages, which the 'sage femmme' assures her will mean that she

> 'will be just like what [she was] before. There will be no trace, no mark, nothing.'
> That, it seems, is her solution. [...]
> And five weeks afterwards there I am, with not one line, not one wrinkle, not one crease.
> And there he is, lying with a ticket tied round his wrist because he died in hospital. And there I am looking down at him, without one line, without one wrinkle, without one crease.... (GMM 51–2)

Here in the life on the margins, the machine-world enters in, orders and erases even the intimacy of motherhood. Even birth and death have become unhomely.

> The sage femme has very white hands and clear, slanting eyes and when she looks at you the world stops rocking about. The clouds are clouds, trees are trees, people are people [...] Don't mix them up again. No, I won't. [...]
> But my heart, heavy as lead, heavy as a stone.
> He has a ticket tied round his wrist because he died. Lying so cold and still with a ticket round his wrist because he died. [...]
> 'God is very cruel,' I said, 'very cruel. A devil, of course. That accounts for everything – the only possible explanation.' (GMM 116–17)

11

Good Night, Day

The cycles of resistance and defeat, self-creation and despair, mockery and mourning, are repeated again and again in this novel. Sasha describes her failed attempt to drink herself to death, after she has been finally disowned on behalf of her family by a nameless 'extremely respectable' relative, since she has had the temerity to stay alive, which in his eyes, no self-respecting fallen woman should do.

> I've had enough of those streets that sweat a cold, yellow slime, of hostile people, of crying myself to sleep every night. [...] I watch myself gradually breaking up – cheeks puffing out, eyes getting smaller. Never mind. [...] Besides, it isn't my face, this tortured and tormented mask. I can take it off whenever I like and hang it up on a nail. Or shall I place on it a tall hat with a green feather, hang a veil over the lot, and walk about the dark streets so merrily? Singing defiantly 'You don't like me, but I don't like you either. "Don't like jam, lamb or ham, and I *don't* like roly-poly...."' Singing 'One more river to cross, that's Jordan, Jordan....'
>
> I have no pride – no pride, no name, no face, no country. I don't belong. I don't belong anywhere. Too sad, too sad...It doesn't matter, there I am, like one of those straws which floats round the edge of a whirlpool, the dead centre, where everything is stagnant, everything is calm. (GMM 37–8)

Despair, defiance, desolation: the condition of the marginal, the unacceptable, those without country, those who don't belong, those caught up in the 'unwinnable war' of the excluded.[1] Sasha is not the only straw in the metropolitan whirlpool. At times *Good Morning, Midnight* can seem the darkest of Rhys's novels, not surprisingly given its date. Its emotional violence and explosiveness, the intensity and brutality of the intolerance it registers, the desperation it charts in those excluded, all suggest Rhys's sense of the coming apocalypse. Perhaps Sasha's lowest moment in the book is when, while sitting drinking in the Deux Magots, she is sucked into 'a misery of utter darkness', seeing the 'whole bloody human race' as a 'pack of damned hyenas'. In a frenzy of paranoia, she thinks,

> ...I know all about myself now, I know. You've told me so often. You haven't left me one rag of illusion to clothe myself in. But by God, I know what you are too, and I wouldn't change places....
>
> Everything spoiled, all spoiled. Well, don't cry about it. No, I won't cry about it.... But may you tear each other to bits, you damned hyenas, and the quicker the better.... Let it be destroyed. Let it happen. Let it end, this cold insanity. Let it happen. (*GMM* 145)

When, at the Exhibition, René (who has just dismissed the Russians as 'Jews and poor whites') sees the Trocadero's Star of Peace, he ominously denounces it as 'mesquin [...] vulgar [...] mesquin, your Star of Peace' (*GMM* 137).

But if Sasha is at her emotional nadir in the Deux Magots, she herself, unlike René, finds a moment of peace, almost hope, at the Trocadero. It is 'cold, empty, beautiful – this is what I imagined, this is what I wanted [...] the cold fountains, the cold, rainbow lights on the water...' (*GMM* 137). Part of the remarkable achievement of Rhys's fiction is that she brings together the terrifying anger and despair of abjection with the impulse of hope, hatred with the longing for human love and tenderness, the brutishness of human existence with its moments of beauty and compassion. Her protagonists recognize that within themselves is 'all. Good, evil, love, hate, life, death, beauty, ugliness' (*SP* 161). That emotional complexity and ambivalence is always intimately related to their impossible position within an intolerant and paranoiac society. Her protagonists are aware of their disempowerment and psychic impairment, aware that the crushing machinery of demarcation goes remorselessly on: the political system which Rhys analyses in her Caribbean and continental fiction is one and the same, a system based on divisions of class, race, money and gender, a system whose underlying cruelty and inhumanity her fiction lays bare. Like the French-Algerian-Jewish Hélène Cixous, Rhys grew up in a colony at the '"height" of imperial blindness', where the colonizers behaved 'in a country that was inhabited by humans as if it were peopled by nonbeings, born-slaves'. Like Cixous, Rhys

learned everything from this first spectacle...how the white...
superior, plutocratic, civilized world founded its power in the
repressions of populations who had suddenly become 'invisible',
like proletarians, immigrant workers, minorities who were not the
right 'color'. Women. Invisible as humans. But of course perceived as
tools – dirty, stupid, lazy, underhanded, etc....The great noble
'advanced' countries established themselves by expelling what was
'strange'; excluding it but not dismissing it; enslaving it. A common-
place gesture of History: there have to be two races – the masters and
the slaves.

We know the implied irony in the master/slave dialectic: the *body* of
what is strange must not disappear, but its force must be conquered
and returned to the master. Both the appropriate and the inappropri-
ate must exist: the clean, hence the dirty, the rich hence the poor.[2]

This last point is of course precisely the one Sasha makes, or
rather does not make, to Mr Blank: 'There must be the dark
background to show up bright colours. Some must cry so that the
others may be able to laugh the more heartily.' The simultaneity
of the exclusion and enslavement of the strange is also one of
Rhys's constant themes. Images of being caged, enslaved,
confined recur throughout her fictions. In this novel Sasha is in
a literal and emotional impasse.[3] She dreams, right at the
beginning, of being lost in the underground with no way out,
'no exit sign'. She is stifled within her anonymous rooms. ('Four
walls, a roof, a bed. *Les Hommes en Cage*...Exactly'.) In her
moments of despair the room becomes a welcome coffin, though
the girl in the bar-tabac, she realizes, is shut away miserably 'in
her coffin' by people like herself (*GMM* 149 and 89). There are just
a few moments when the world opens out. Here in the Trocadero;
when she reaches Paris with Enno – 'A door has opened and let
me into the sun' (*GMM* 104); when she looks at Serge's paintings
– 'Now the room expands and the iron band round my heart
loosens. The miracle has happened. I am happy' (*GMM* 838).

Yet, in spite of Sasha's pervading sense of confined impotence,
in spite of the power of 'organized society' against which, like
Julia, she so often feels she has not 'a dog's chance' (*ALM* 17), in
spite of the psychic turmoil and fragmentation she describes,
Rhys shows Sasha, in Paula Le Gallez's words, remaining 'in
narrative control'.[4] Although Sasha thinks at one moment that a
book (this book perhaps) called *Just a Cérébrale or you can't stop me*

from dreaming would only be accepted as authentic if by a man, although as a ghost writer for a rich woman she was forced to abandon her own chosen words, here she speaks, here she gives her view of the eyes that try to transfix her in their gaze. The novel ends ambiguously, like *Wide Sargasso Sea*. Is Antoinette the destroyed or the destroyer as she burns down the English house? Has Sasha surrendered to self-hatred or achieved human compassion in her embrace of the commis at the end of *Good Morning, Midnight*? There is no escape from irredeemable ambivalence, no certain closure. But closure in terms of plot is not the point. What matters is that her narrative asserts, to the end, her dissent from the machine's version of the truth.

12

The Struggle for the Sign

I want to end with some further comments on Rhys's 'struggle for the sign', and the nature and form of the counter-discourse which she evolves. Like other postmodernist and postcolonialist writers – and whilst those two categories by no means always coincide, many of their strategies do – Rhys in her fictions unpicks and mocks the language by which the powerful keep control, while at the same time shifting, bending, re-inventing ways of using language to open up fresh possibilities of being. She questions and destabilizes the hegemonic language which seeks to define her in its terms, rewriting, in her Creole hand, the metropolitan script. As Spivak puts it, 'in post-coloniality, every metropolitan definition is dislodged. The general mode for the post-colonial is citation, re-inscription, re-routing the historical.'[1] Rhys 'protest[s] loudly' in her fiction, as she did in the Bromley courtroom, against intolerance and injustice, yet at the same time she recreates and reshapes language to map the unknown and uncharted world of ambivalence. Both protest and creation are integral to her writing, one of whose distinctive features is its fusion of apparently contrary elements – rage and reverie, farce and feeling, speech and poetry, satirical critique and psychic depth. If the melancholy haze through which her work is too often read has led critics to simplify and sentimentalize the psychology of her heroines, it has even more obscured the fact that she is a savagely funny writer, a witty and incisive deconstructionist, whose deconstruction is a necessary part of her struggle to find a narrative form through which to chart the subjectivity of those on the margins.[2] The old Jew in *Good Morning, Midnight*, with his banjo and mocking, tender, painful songs, is perhaps an image of the kind of artist Rhys is herself, her version of Wallace Stevens' 'Man with the Blue Guitar'. Indeed, perhaps Serge's art as a whole is an image of hers. Like Rhys, he is an outsider, who paints outsiders: just as he/Rhys tells the story of the mulatto woman's suffering, so his paintings portray society's outcasts, the old Jew in the gutter, misshapen dwarfs, prostitutes old and young. And if his paintings, like Rhys's stories, tell the tale of those on the margins, his masks are the equivalent, as well as the purveyor, of her satire.

Masks are frequently vehicles for satire in Rhys's fiction. Helen Tiffin, and later Mary-Lou Emery, have suggested that the grotesque masks Rhys saw in the Dominican carnival as a child, and which she describes in *Smile Please* and *Voyage in the Dark*, are the source of their pervasive presence in her texts. These masks were simultaneously subversive and frightening, masks from behind which the black dancers could mock the whites, but to the child terrifying simulations of power. In Rhys's fiction, several very different sorts of masks appear, but most often she writes of masks assumed by the powerful to terrorize the weak.[3] And just as mirrors in her fiction, I earlier suggested, are intimately connected with language, so these masks are verbal as well as visual. Just as, in *Three Guineas*, Virginia Woolf points to the patriarchal, militarist power which parades behind ritualistic façades of uniforms and medals, so Rhys exposes not just the uniforms of 'bowler hat, majestic trousers', but the empty, tyrannical pomposity of the codes and clichés by which organized society enforces its domination: for example, a code like Mr Mackenzie's, which

> was perfectly adapted to the social system and [which] in any argument he could have defended against any attack whatsoever. However, he never argued about it, because that was part of the code. You didn't argue about these things. Simply, under certain circumstances you did this, and under other circumstances you did that. (*ALM* 18)

Even the convention-bound upper-middle-class lovers in Rhys's stories are at times presented as 'poor devil[s] of [...] human being[s]' (*GMM* 158): Mr Mackenzie's guilty secret is that he published a book of poetry in his youth, which he blames for 'the kink in his nature' which against all the dictates of his code 'morbidly attracted him to strangeness, to recklessness, even unhappiness' (*ALM* 18–19). But when these men retreat behind the clichés which defend their self-interest they enter the world of caricature and farce. 'Mr Blank' is pure satire – he need be no more than a caricature because he only appears as the agent of a system which is a caricature of humanity in itself. When, in *Quartet*, Heidler turns up in a bowler hat, looking 'exactly like a picture of Queen Victoria', Rhys ridicules his explanation to Marya that

> one had to keep up appearances. That everybody had to. Everybody had for everybody's sake to keep up appearances. It was everybody's duty, it was in fact what they were there for.

> 'You've got to play the game.' (*Q* 89)

Given this account of his ontological beliefs, it is not surprising that Marya later visualizes Heidler saying, as he leaves church,

> God's a pal of mine. [...] He probably looks rather like me, with cold eyes and fattish hands. I'm in His image or He's in mine. It's all one. I prayed to Him to get you and I got you. Shall I give you a letter of introduction? Yes, I might do that if you remind me. No trouble at all. Now then, don't be hysterical. Besides, Lois was there first. Lois is a good woman and you are a bad one; it's quite simple. These things are. That's what's meant by having principles. Nobody owes a fair deal to a prostitute. It isn't done. My dear girl, what would become of things if it were? Come, come to think it over. Intact or not intact, that's the first question. An income or not an income, that's the second. (*Q* 125)

Rhys takes a Durkheimian view of God – He's made in the image of the social system to give authority to the social system: as Julia thinks bitterly about Neil James: 'Because he has money he's a kind of god. Because I have none I'm a kind of worm' (*ALM* 81). Principles in this world, according to Rhys, mean those simple rules that guard the interests of those receiving interest – an analysis which could be presented as positively Marxist, though, as I suggested earlier, Rhys has a much more Foucauldian concept of power than a Marxist one, and certainly a more Foucauldian concept of language. She repeatedly shows her protagonists disputing the way language is used as an instrument by the strong against the weak. As Anna in *Voyage in the Dark* says, after she has lost her virginity, 'I am bad, not good any longer, bad. That has no meaning, absolutely none. Just words. But something about the darkness of the streets has a meaning' (*VD* 49). The darkness of the streets, the actuality of being a penniless woman alone in Edwardian London, are in another dimension, inexpressible, inadmissible in the language of bourgeois morality. In Heidler's language, Marya's human needs disappear. In what sense can Marya be described, not as a lover, but as a 'prostitute', to whom no 'fair deal' is owed? Only in the sense that because she has no money, Heidler can only have his affair with her by also providing financial support – which means, according to the rules of his game, his sole obligation is to do with money. Because Marya is poor, he can ignore her feelings. When she cracks under the emotional strain, he presumes 'it's a question of money. I rather thought that was what you were getting at' (Q 81). It is then that she hits him.

For organized society, morality and money are inseparable terms. ('Intact or not intact, that's the first question. An income or not an income, that's the second.') As Anna lunches with her stepmother, fearing Hester will discover she's now a kept woman, she cannot take her eyes from an advertisement at the back of a fellow luncher's newspaper: 'What is Purity? For Thirty-Five Years the Answer has been Bourne's Cocoa' (VD 50). Purity is material rather than metaphysical in this world: sure enough, her stepmother is quite prepared to ignore her dubious position if it means she can evade supporting Anna. The same goes for aesthetics when Sasha is assured the hotel offers 'beautiful rooms' she thinks bitterly

> A beautiful room with bath? A room with bath? A nice room? A room? ... But never tell the truth about this business of rooms, because it would bust the roof off everything and undermine the whole social system. All rooms are the same. All rooms have four walls, a door, a window or two, a bed, a chair and perhaps a bidet. A room is a place where you hide from the wolves outside and that's all any room is. (GMM 33)

Rhys's protagonists are acutely aware that the social machine is kept in place by a use of language which ignores nuance, complexity, deviation, ambivalence, a language which reiterates the fetishistic phrases which preserve the status quo. Sasha thinks of her family's moralizing:

> These phrases run trippingly off the tongues of the extremely respectable. They think in terms of a sentimental ballad. And that's what terrifies you about them. It isn't their cruelty, it isn't even their

shrewdness – it's their extraordinary naïveté. Everything in their whole bloody world is a cliché. Everything is born out of a cliché, rests on a cliché, survives by a cliché. And they believe in the clichés – there's no hope. (*GMM* 36)

In *Wide Sargasso Sea*, too tragic a text for satire, but full of irony, Antoinette says to her husband:

Justice [...] I've heard that word. It's a cold word. I tried it out...I wrote it down several times and always it looked a damn cold lie to me. There is no justice. [...] My mother [...] what justice did she have? (*WSS* 121)

As Mr Severn thinks morosely in 'Tigers are Better Looking', 'what is wanted [...] is a brand-new lot of words' (*TABL* 73).

One cannot have a brand-new lot of words, but it is possible to get beyond the clichés, to explore ambiguity, difference, darkness, warmth. Part of the modernist project was to find ways of making words do brand-new things. Language, in the world of Chambers' postmodern migrants, 'is appropriated, taken apart, and then put back together with a new inflection, an unexpected accent, a further twist in the tale'. Perhaps, as Kristeva says of all those subject to the abject, migrants have as their 'symptom...the rejection and reconstruction of languages'.[4] Rhys rejects the language of empire, of colonialism, of class, of bourgeois morality, and constructs a different one. Language is not only the empty code that keeps injustice in place by claiming it is justice: it is the one tool one has to make alternative sense of the world. As Hélène Cixous has said, 'Writing is precisely the *very possibility of change*, the space that can serve as a springboard for subversive thought, the precursory movement, of a transformation of social and cultural structures'.[5]

'Oh, the relief of words!' Rhys wrote in the Ropemaker's Diary (*SP* 165). Rhys's sense of what writing could do brings one back to the question of the connection between her autobiography and her fiction. She wrote in a notebook some time in the mid-thirties:

It was so intolerable this longing this sadness I got from the shapes of the mountains, the sound of the rain the moment just after sunset that one day I spoke to my mother of it and she at once gave me a large dose of castor oil.

One day I discovered I could work off the worst of it by writing poems and was happier.[6]

81

Much later, in an interview in *Mademoiselle* in 1974, she was asked about the connection between the pain of her life and her books, in particular the baby who dies in *Good Morning, Midnight*. Rhys replied:

> My son did die. It made a terrible impression on me and I had to bring it in. I think it was Somerset Maugham who said that if you write out a thing, it goes ... and it doesn't trouble you so much. You're left with a vague melancholy, but not utter misery. I suppose it's like psychoanalysis or a Catholic going to confession.[7]

She is clearly thinking of Freud's own modest claim to turn neurotic misery into ordinary human unhappiness, but these comments are very much the kind that have on the one hand fuelled reductively personalized readings of her work and on the other alarmed more traditional literary critics, still edgily aware of New Critical strictures against romantic self-indulgence. Even her interviewer here (who had earlier written, 'I had suspected, in fact assumed, that Jean Rhys had based her novels on her life') responded in alarm: 'but that kind of writing is often autobiographical spew. Yours has form, precision.'[8]

Rhys's work does have form and precision, but there are perhaps other ways to look at the analogy between fiction and psychoanalytic practice. Form and precision are not necessarily incompatible with the search to find a meaningful way to turn traumas into tales, and if the traumas grow out of an as yet unexplored history, they have to be new forms, precise in different ways. Rhys believed, like George Bernanos, whom she quoted in another letter to Morchard Bishop, that

> *'Il faudrait parler de soi avec une rigeur inflexible.'* [...]
> I know that 'parler de soi' is not supposed to be the proper thing to do. Not in England. And not now in 1953.
> I feel so fiercely about that. No one knows anything but himself or herself. And that badly.
> Don't you think so? Other people are seen and heard and felt. Known? Not on your life. (JRL 103–4)[9]

It is, perhaps, the rigour which counts in this search to understand the self. Unless, like Sasha's relatives, one echoes a sentimental ballad, telling a life entails wrestling with shape and sense, always a problematic business. Putting together the story of a life is not easy, as Julia finds, to Mr Horsfield's tense disapproval.

> She spoke as if she were trying to recall a book she had read or a story she had heard and Mr Horsfield felt irritated by her vagueness, 'because' he thought, 'your life is your life, and you must be pretty definite about it. Or if it's a story you are making up, you ought at least to have it pat.' (*ALM* 38–9)

But the story which Julia has begun, he finds, is the story of the problems of telling her life-story. She attempted to tell it to a woman sculptor for whom she modelled, but the woman didn't believe her:

> It was a beastly feeling I got – that I didn't quite believe myself either... I felt as if all my life and all myself were floating away from me like smoke and there was nothing to lay hold of – nothing [...] it was [...] like looking over the edge of the world [...] I wanted to say [...] But who am I then? [...] and how did I get here? [...] When I got home I pulled out all the photographs I had, and letters and things [...] but it had all gone, as if it had never been [...] then I was frightened, and yet I knew if I could get to the end of what I was feeling it would be the truth about myself and about the world and about everything that one puzzles and pains about all the time. (*ALM* 41)

In Rhys's novels, as in psychoanalysis, it is through the pain of the destabilization of identity, and through the destabilization of language, that the truth can be found. If, as I have argued, Rhys is giving an account of a kind of subjectivity 'never before so accurately described', she had to evolve her own narrative form and her own concept of the psyche, which perhaps, as in psychoanalysis, were inseparable.

In an essay exploring the links between the analytic experience and the novel, Kristeva talks of writing as 'a semiotic practice that facilitates the ultimate reorganisation of psychic space'. In particular, she says, the novel form, like the adolescent psyche, 'opens itself to the repressed at the same time that it initiates a psychic reorganisation of the individual'.[10] Opening oneself to the repressed is perhaps one way of describing what Julia is doing when she tries to follow her terror at the dissolution of her identity to 'the end', and a way of describing the narrative strategy of Rhys's fiction. The aim of psychoanalysis is, after all, to enable the analysand to tell a story, a story which makes life comprehensible and therefore bearable, to find a narrative which makes sense of the disparate pieces of a life when 'all life' seems, as it does to Marya, 'a dream. . . A dream. *La vie toute faite des morceaux. Sans suite comme des rêves'* (*Q* 96).

Rhys, like most writers, took some time to evolve her own particular form. Her short stories in *The Left Bank* have already her very selective use of detail and her emphasis on subjectivity, but transitions of consciousness and time tend to be quite conventionally handled. 'Vienne' is the one which gives most indication of how her technique would develop. It begins, 'Funny how it's slipped away, Vienna. Nothing left but a few snapshots', and is presented as a sequence of apparently disconnected memories – fragments, often retold in fragmentary sentences, but a sequence of intensely realized subjective moments. These fragments each give different glimpses of women in relationship to men and to their sexuality – sometimes women whom the narrator Frances has known, sometimes different phases of herself – that trying on of provisional, partial identities which is incorporated into so many later Rhys texts. *Quartet*, the first novel, goes back to a more traditional form: the whole is shaped in that classic nineteenth-century genre, the novel of adultery. Looking back from her later fiction, it seems oddly rigid at times. Marya's past is explained by the authorial narrator, connecting links are offered which in her later novels would be assumed. It has a much more definite plot than her other novels: the changes Rhys has made from her own life (Heidler's marriage, Stephan's crime) are all in the direction of *solidity*, that novelistic quality Marya herself recognizes her background sadly lacks. It is not for nothing this is the only Rhys novel to have been filmed by Merchant-Ivory. In *After Leaving Mr Mackenzie*, in which Julia thinks of the novel's events as 'a disconnected episode to be placed with all the other disconnected episodes' of her life (*ALM* 119), Rhys is already moving towards her characteristic mingling of past and present, the fantasized and the factual. Julia's drifting, disorientated present, her humiliation at her rejection by Mr Mackenzie, her painful re-encounter with her disapproving family at the time of her mother's death, reawaken memories of the past: of the time when her mother was still the 'sweet, warm centre of the world', of her childhood when trees were friendly or at least not hostile, of 'the last time you were happy about nothing; the first time you were afraid about nothing' (*ALM* 78 and 116). But this interpenetration is first fully achieved in *Voyage in the Dark*, in which Jean Rhys said she was trying to show

Something to do with time being an illusion I think. I mean the past exists – side by side with the present, not behind it; that what was – is.

I tried to do it by making the past (the West Indies) very vivid – the present dreamlike (downward career of the girl) – starting of course piano and ending fortissimo.

Perhaps I was simply trying to describe a girl going potty. (JRL, 24)

None of Rhys's work was published until she was thirty-four, but she had been writing about her life since she was a young girl. *Voyage in the Dark* was first written as an autobiographical account, as was 'Vienne'. I would suggest it was from her questing, discontinuous, self-interrogating journal writing that she in fact developed the style that works so powerfully in her fiction. Rhys's novels, particularly her last three, have much in common with the language of the analysand. They are fragmented, weave backwards and forwards, follow associations, circle back again and again to certain events, certain phrases. The narrators recall dreams, images, fantasies: they experience past as powerfully as, more intensely than the present, turn memories of looks and feelings into words. Even the narrative events that form the present of the novels are often akin to a series of vivid memories – 'Quickly, while I can', Antoinette says at one moment, 'I must remember the hot classroom' (*WSS* 44). Their narratives follow the twists and shifts of a divided, self-reflexive consciousness, and, while there may be no resolution or closure in conventional terms what does emerge are symbolic patterns, a reformed symbolic order; the fictions find their shape, a shape which is in itself a 'reorganisation of psychic space'.[12]

Yet although Rhys's fiction is so concerned with subjectivity, it is not, as I have argued, simply inward-looking. For all her protagonists, as for Julia, what most profoundly destabilizes their identity is the clash between how they are seen and how they see, how they are labelled and how they might speak. They all live inner lives of psychic extremity, but even if they are 'perhaps [...] going potty', that inner turmoil is a register of their fraught position in the world. For Rhys to make sense of existences like hers meant understanding the historical and social forces which had made them what they are. In 'The Day They Burned the Books' she draws on the material of her life and uses it transformed, to understand how colonialism shapes the psyches of colonized and colonizer. In *Good Morning, Midnight*, she draws on the material of her life once more, on her own displacement and loss, to explore the consciousness of those under threat – and of those threatening – in the paranoiac world of 1937. The same process is at work in all her fiction. It is impossible to separate her readings of the psyches of those whose lives are misshapen and coerced by the hierarchical machinery of organized society from her analysis of the working of that machinery itself. As I have attempted to show, she constantly, in Bhabha's words, 'relat[es] the traumatic ambivalences of a personal, psychic history to the wider disjunctions of political existence'.

I talked earlier about the multiple voices in Rhys's texts, voices remembered, inner dialogue, indirect speech. Whether her narratives are third or first person, they are always a collage of texts, echoes of conversations, songs, advertisements, poetry, law reports, quotations from books, letters, even prayers: in short, postmodernist fictions, told by a narrative voice or voices which re-inscribe, re-invent, resist and transform the multiple stories into which, as Lyotard says, we are all born. Rhys's language fuses these other discourses with the syntax and vocabulary of speech, yet, her style, in its rhythmic repetition of imagery and phrases, is highly poetic. For example, Antoinette's account of life at the convent, in which the prayers and the answers of the nuns are drawn into the flow:

> The long brown room was full of gold sunlight and shadows of trees moving quietly. I learnt to say very quickly as the others did, 'offer up all the prayers, works and sufferings of this day.' But what about happiness, I thought at first, is there no happiness? There must be. Oh happiness, of course, happiness, well.
>
> But I soon forgot about happiness, running down the stairs to the big stone bath where we splashed about wearing long grey cotton chemises which reached to our ankles. The smell of soap as you cautiously soaped yourself under the chemise, a trick to be learnt, dressing with modesty, another trick. Great splashes of sunlight as we ran up the wooden steps of the refectory. Hot coffee and rolls and melting butter. But after the meal, now and at the hour of our death, and at midday, and at six in the evening, now and at the hour of our death. Let perpetual Light shine on them. This is for my mother, I would think, wherever her mind is wandering, for it has left her body. Then I remembered how she hated a strong light and loved the cool and the shade. It is a different light they told me. Still I would not say it. (*WSS* 47)

The convent is the kindliest of the authorities which Antoinette meets, but even there she interrogates and reforms their liturgy, sifting and shifting its meanings. Her account is built around the oxymoron of her first description of the convent as 'a place of sunlight and death' (WSS 47). But it is not just in the convent that 'everything was brightness, or dark . . . sun or shadow, Heaven or Hell' (WSS 48). Throughout Wide Sargasso Sea the imagery juxtaposes light and dark, pain and desire, beauty and death, from the moment, right at the beginning, when Antoinette finds their horse poisoned under the frangipani tree, to the final flame which lights her 'along the dark passage' to the burning of the house and her death (WSS 156).

Rhys had originally, she told Diana Athill, intended to begin and end Wide Sargasso Sea with a dream, while the rest would have been 'a long monologue. Antoinette in her prison room remembers, loves, hates, raves, talks to imaginary people, hears imaginary voices answering and overhears meaningless conversations outside' (JRL, 233). She wrote quite an amount of the novel in this way, but although she kept much of this version in the final draft, she decided against continuing. She had had battles over her original conclusion of Voyage in the Dark: in the end there was not so much of Anna 'going potty' as Rhys had intended, as her publisher persuaded her to cut by half the delirious memories of childhood in Part Four. Her plan for Wide Sargasso Sea, she feared, would be even more unacceptable. 'No-one will get the hang of [it] . . . "A mad girl speaking all the time is too much! " '(JRL, 233). Such a novel would have been, one guesses, a powerful and innovative work, and in one sense a natural evolution of her technique. But so was the shape she finally found: two subjectivities so tragically besieged, in their different ways, by the terrifying forces of colonial bitterness; two narrative voices, each echoing, parrying, questioning the voices around them. The Rochester figure ('dreadful man, but I tried to be fair') (JRL, 233) is no simple brute: he too, like Antoinette, loves, hates and raves. But in the end he takes the English, colonial, masculinist way out of his pain, suppression of the emotional, oppression of the other. Even so, it is a struggle. The voices that leap into his mind jar or mock him – they appear in the text as separate italicized sentences, unlike the voices which Antoinette fuses into her own thought. He is a study in the process of repression:

87

Antoinette opens herself to the repressed. She may be driven mad, but in Toni Morrison's words, this is 'going mad in order not to lose your mind'. Like Sasha she never finally succumbs to the metropolitan judgements. She knows what she thinks of their justice: she is sure of the worthlessness of its 'cardboard world [...] that has no light in it' (*WSS* 148). 'Time', she says, 'has no meaning', but her red dress, 'the colour of fire and sunsets' 'the colour of flamboyant flowers', the colour of the dress she wore when she last saw her lover Sandi, 'that has a meaning' (*WSS* 151). As Louis James put it, 'At the end, she asserts the value of heat and light against the darkness. Jean Rhys does not show us her death. We are left with the image of her carrying the flickering light down the dark corridor that cannot overcome it.'[13] Rochester's hate may have been 'colder, stronger' (JRL, 140), but Antoinette has the last word.

Rhys's poetic use of the spoken voice has perhaps affinities with Toni Morrison's writing. Morrison is very consciously creating a counter-discourse which draws on black oral traditions, and these may to some extent lie behind Rhys's language too. When Rhys first came to England she had a strong West Indian accent – as does Anna, to whom Hester says: 'That awful sing-song voice you had! Exactly like a nigger you talked – and still do' (*VD* 56). It was Rhys's accent, according to Carole Angier, which was the real reason for her having to give up her attempts to be an actress. Soon she began to speak in a whisper: people could hardly hear what she said.[14] The effect of the prejudice she met was, almost literally, to silence her, until she found her voice as a writer. Yet the musicality of Caribbean rhythms can still be found in her writing – 'being black is warm and gay, being white is cold and sad' (*VD* 27) – particularly in the richly evoked language of her black characters, like Christophine in *Wide Sargasso Sea* or Selina in 'Let Them Call it Jazz'. Her construction of the language of her novels as speech – uncertain, fragmented speech – pits the response of the individual, the marginal, the dispossessed, the colonized, against the public, the hegemonic, the discourse of power, the language of empire.[15] In the sense that the feminine is the place of disempowerment and of the unspoken it is a feminized use of language. In her novels she writes back to an intolerant society which despises difference. In the Ropemaker's Diary, she constructs 'The Trial of Jean Rhys', which shows her movement from defeat and failure in life to her writing.

> Defence. *Did you make great efforts to, shall we say, establish contacts with other people? I mean friendships, love affairs, so on?*
> Yes. Not friendships very much.
> Did you succeed?
> Sometimes. For a time.
> *It didn't last?*
> No.
> *Whose fault was that?*
> Mine I suppose
> *You suppose?*
> Silence.
> *Better answer.*
> I am tired. I learnt everything too late. Everything was always one jump ahead of me.
> *The phrase is not 'I do not know' but 'I have nothing to say'.*
> The trouble is I have plenty to say. Not only that but I am bound to say it.
> *Bound?*
> I must.
> *Why? Why? Why?*
> I must write. (*SP* 162–3)

It is at that point that the words appear which I quoted at the beginning of this book. 'If I stop writing my life will have been an abject failure. It is that already to other people. But it could be an abject failure to myself. I will not have earned death' (*SP* 163).

By the time Jean Rhys met that well-earned death, she was famous and her work acclaimed. Yet the depth and complexity of her work as a whole has only come to be recognized in the last few years. Paul Theroux, reviewing the republished *After Leaving Mr Mackenzie* in 1972, asked whether Rhys's 'placelessness' had held up her 'public recognition'.[16] As Naipaul said, as far as the Europeans were concerned, she came from nowhere. Yet now, perhaps, it is the recognition of what she has to say about displacement, dislocation and loss which makes her work seem so relevant today. Coming from the fissured and ambivalent world of the colonial margins, with their torn and violent history, to the grim, chill edges of metropolitan society, she was able to forge a powerful critique of European values and hierarchies, and to give new insights into the darkness, frailty, pain, desire and hope within the human psyche.

Notes

INTRODUCTION

1. Angier, 446. Unless other sources are cited, biographical information about Jean Rhys is drawn from Carole Angier's biography (*Jean Rhys*) or from Jean Rhys's letters (*Letters*, 1931–1966). I have found the information in Angier's biography invaluable, though I do not always interpret events as she does. Jean Rhys's life in Beckenham is covered in Angier, 440–57. I should point out that when Jean Rhys said 'English', she meant English, not British. She felt quite differently about the Welsh, Scottish and Irish.
2. Rachel Bowlby, 'The Impasse', in *Still Crazy After All These Years* (London: Routledge, 1993), 34.
3. Quoted in Iain Chambers, *Migrancy, Culture, Identity* (London: Routledge, 1994), 1.

CHAPTER 1. JEAN RHYS AND HER CRITICS

1. See Elgin W. Mellown, *Jean Rhys: a Descriptive and Annotated Bibliography of Works and Criticism* (New York and London: Garland Publishing, 1984), 6, 9, 11, 39–40 and 41.
2. Mellown, 10, 24, 39. The three comments come from, respectively, a review of *Postures* (the title under which *Quartet* was first published) in *The Bookman* in 1929, a review of *After Leaving Mr Mackenzie* in the *TLS* in 1931, and a review of *Voyage in the Dark* in *Harper's Bazaar* in 1934.
3. 'Boule de Suif', a short story by Guy de Maupassant, has a plot as summarized by Rhys here, but with French rather than British housewives.
4. 'La Maison Tellier', again by Maupassant, is a short story set in a brothel.
5. Judith Kegan Gardiner, 'Good Morning, Midnight; Good Night, Modernism', *Boundary 2*, 11 (Fall–Winter, 1982–3), 242.

6. Mary Cantwell, 'A Conversation with Jean Rhys' (1974), reprinted in Pierrette Frickey (ed.), (Washington, DC: Three Continents Press, 1990), 23.

7. Al Alvarez, 'The Best Living Novelist', *New York Times Review of Books*, 17 March 1974, pp. 6–7.

8. Quoted by Elgin Mellown in 'Characters and Themes in the Novels of Jean Rhys', in Frickey, 106.

9. Frickey, 106. Mellown's brief quotation from Stella Bowen allows for a significant misreading of her point: she is not saying that Rhys was actually a victim, but, with understandable resentment, that that was how she was seen. The passage goes: 'Life with Ford always felt pretty insecure ... Yet here I was cast for the role of the fortunate wife who held all the cards, and the girl for that of the poor, brave and desperate beggar who was doomed to be let down by the bourgeoisie. I learnt what a powerful weapon lies in weakness and pathos and how strong is the position of the person who has nothing to lose, and I simply hated my role' (Angier 143).

10. Jean Rhys, 'Making Bricks without Straw', in Frickey, 35.

11. In fact, Carter, unlike me, does see Jean Rhys's characters as Justine's grandchildren, p. 56.

12. In *Good Morning, Midnight*, Sasha's hotel is in an 'impasse' – French for no-through or dead-end road – and Rachel Bowlby has tellingly explored its symbolism for Sasha's state of mind: see Bowlby.

13. Jacqueline Rose, *The Haunting of Sylvia Plath* (London: Virago, 1991), 17.

14. See, for example, Angier, 218, and Gail Pool, reviewing *Smile Please*, in the *Chicago Review* in 1981, quoted in Mellown, *Jean Rhys*, 121.

15. See the blurbs for the Penguin editions of *Quartet, After Leaving Mr Mackenzie, Wide Sargasso Sea* and *Smile Please*.

16. David Plante, *Difficult Women: a Memoir of Three* (London: Gollanz, 1983), 45.

17. Plante, 45.

18. Among others Rhys refers to in her letters and fiction are Milton, Swift, Wordsworth, Keats, Shelley, Mallarmé, Verlaine, Anatole France, Alphonse Daudet, Edgar Allan Poe, Thackeray, Christina Rossetti, George Borrow, George Moore, Rider Haggard, Rudyard Kipling, Knut Hamsun, Henry James, Conrad, Joyce, Katherine Mansfield, Kafka, Hemingway, Scott Fitzgerald, H. E. Bates, Jean Genet, Colette, Jean Cocteau, Sartre, Christopher Isherwood, Zola, Martha Gellhorn, J. D. Salinger, Stevie Smith ('a great favourite of mine', *Letters*, 122), Arthur Koestler, Carson McCullers, Denton Welch, Oscar Wilde. It is true that the letters cover little before the Second World War, but, in addition to Ford's testimony, her ex-husband Jean Lenglet, in an article written under his pseudonym

Edward de Nève in *Les Nouvelles Littéraires*, no. 880, 26 August 1939, describes her in London reading all the important books published in England, America and France (Mellown, *Jean Rhys*, p. 168). The one period when she appears to have stopped reading was at the time of her first affair.

19. 'Good Morning, Midnight', Gardiner, 234. In *Good Morning, Midnight* there are also references to the German Romantic poet Heine and to Aeschylus's *Eumenides*, the latter spotted by Peter Wolfe (see his *Jean Rhys*), who describes it quite inaccurately as a 'rare literary allusion'.

20. Coral Ann Howells, *Jean Rhys* (Hemel Hempstead: Harvester Wheatsheaf, 1991), 38.

21. Alvarez, 7: 'no axes to grind, no ideas to tout', he continues.

CHAPTER 2. FEMINIST AND POSTCOLONIAL APPROACHES TO JEAN RHYS

1. Early feminist responses include Rosalind Miles, *The Fiction of Sex: Themes and Function of Sex Difference in the Modern Novel* (London: Vision Press, 1974); Judith Thurman, 'The Mistress and the Mask: Jean Rhys's Fiction, *Ms* 4 (January, 1976), 50–2, 91; Helen Tiffin, 'Mirror and Mask: Colonial Motifs in Novels of Jean Rhys', 17 (April 1978), 328–341; Elizabeth Abel, 'Women and Schizophrenia: the Fiction of Jean Rhys', *Contemporary Literature*, 20 (Spring 1979), 155–77. The first full-length feminist account was Helen Nebeker's *Jean Rhys: Woman in Passage: a Critical Study of the Novels of Jean Rhys* (Montreal, Canada: Eden Press, 1981).

2. Helen McNeill, reviewing *Smile Please* in *New Statesman*, 99 (15 February 1980), in Mellown, *Jean Rhys*, 53.

3. Rachel Blau DuPlessis does not mention Rhys at all in her collections of essays on women and modernism, *The Pink Guitar: Writing as Feminist Practice* (London: Routledge, 1990), and has only a couple of pages on *Wide Sargasso Sea* in *Writing Beyond the Ending: Narrative Strategies of Twentieth-Century Women Writers* (Bloomington: Indiana University Press, 1985), 45–6. Rhys appears only in lists or in the briefest references in Sandra M. Gilbert and Susan Gubar, *No Man's Land: the Place of the Woman Writer in the Twentieth Century*, 3 vols. (New Haven: Yale University Press, 1988, 1989, 1994).

4. Perhaps, for Gubar and Gilbert, Rhys constitutes a particular problem. Their best-selling work, *The Madwoman in the Attic* (New Haven: Yale University Press, 1979), must, partially at least, owe its focus to *Wide Sargasso Sea*, which had so powerfully transformed the figure of the first Mrs Rochester, but it must also fear the novel as its

shadow: their book's celebration of *Jane Eyre* as the paradigmatic feminist text ignores Rhys's critique of its chauvinism.

5. Benstock is inaccurate about Jean Lenglet's offence, which was irregular currency dealing: it was Stephan Zelli in *Quartet* who had been trafficking in stolen goods – precisely the mistake which Diana Athill points out in her foreword to *Smile Please* was made in one of Rhys's obituaries (*SP* 9).

6. Kenneth Ramchand, *The West Indian Novel and Its Background* (London: Faber and Faber, 1970), 33.

7. Ramchand, 36.

8. See, for example, Syed Hussein Alatas, *The Myth of the Lazy Native: a Study of the Image of the Malays, Filipinos and Javanese from the 16th to the 20th Century and its function in the ideology of colonial capitalism* (London: Cass, 1977) and Rana Kabbani, *Europe's Myths of the Orient* (London: Pandora, 1986).

9. Ramchand, 32.

10. Coral Ann Howells, 20.

11. The first to discuss *Wide Sargasso Sea* as a Caribbean novel was Wally Look Lai (in 'The Road to Thornfield Hall: An Analysis of *Wide Sargasso Sea*', *New Beacon Reviews: Collection One*, ed. John La Rose, London: New Beacon Books, 1968), though in 1949 Alec Waugh (Evelyn Waugh's brother), who had met Jean Rhys in England, wrote in his book *The Sugar Islands* that he 'could see how Dominica had coloured her temperament and outlook' (quoted in Mellown, *Jean Rhys*, p. 189), and in 1967, Neville Braybrooke, writing in the *Spectator*, had drawn attention to her West Indian origins (see note 5 to chapter 3). See also Ramchand (1970); Nancy Casey (1973 – see note 16); John Hearne, 'The Wide Sargasso Sea: a West Indian Reflection' in the *Cornhill Magazine*, 1080 (Summer 1974); Louis James 'Sun Fire – Painted Fire: Jean Rhys as a Caribbean Novelist', *Ariel*, 8:3 (1977); Elaine Campbell, 'A Report from Dominica, BWI', in *World Literature Written in English*, 17 (April 1978). The first full-length book to be written on Rhys's work was Louis James's *Jean Rhys* (London: Longman, 1978), which approached her as a Caribbean writer. Although he concentrates on her as a Caribbean, he has had the distinction, for a male critic writing in 1978, of being attacked for *too* feminist an interpretation of her work – see Laura Niesen de Abruna, 'Jean Rhys's Feminism: Theory against Practice', *World Literature Written in English*, 28:2 (1988), 326.

12. V. S. Naipaul, 'Without a Dog's Chance' (1972), in Frickey, 54.

13. Frickey, 58.

14. Kenneth Ramchand has edited a collection of her West Indian stories, *Tales of the Wide Caribbean* (London and Kingston, Jamaica: Heinemann, 1985). (Rhys wrote more about the Caribbean as she

grew older: in her last collection of stories, *Sleep It Off Lady*, eight of sixteen stories have a Caribbean theme; in her first, *The Left Bank*, only three out of twenty-two). Helen Tiffin is one of those who see her colonial origins affecting all her writing, as is Louis James.

15. Kamau Brathwaite, in *Contradictory Omens* (1974), quoted in Mary-Lou Emery, *Jean Rhys at 'World's End': Novels of Colonial and Sexual Exile* (Austin: University of Texas Press, 1990), 19, and in Peter Hulme's 'The Locked Heart; the Creole Family Romance of *Wide Sargasso Sea*', in *Colonial Discourse/Postcolonical Theory*, ed. Francis Barker, Peter Hulme and Margaret Iversen (Manchester and New York: Manchester University Press, 1994), 74. See also Peter Hulme, 'The Place of *Wide Sargasso Sea*', in *Wasafiri*, 20 (Autumn 1994).

16. The first woman as far as I know was Nancy Casey in 'Study in the Alienation of a Creole Woman: Jean Rhys's *Voyage in the Dark* (*Caribbean Quarterly*, no. 19, September 1973, pp. 95–102), which in spite of the title's emphasis on gender, is not a particularly feminist account.

17. Wally Look Lai, 40.

18. See, for example, Bowlby; Sue Roe, 'The Shadow of Light: the Symbolic Underworld of Jean Rhys', in *Women Reading Women Writing*, ed. Sue Roe (Brighton: Harvester, 1987);. Nancy Harrison, *Jean Rhys and the Novel as Women's Text* (Chapel Hill and London: University of North Carolina Press, 1988); Carol R. Hagley, 'Ageing in the Fiction of Jean Rhys', *World Literature Written in English*, 28:1 (1988); Deborah Kelly Kloepfler, *The Unspeakable Mother: Forbidden Discourse in Jean Rhys and HD* (Ithaca and London: Cornell University Press, 1989); Molly Hite, *The Other Side of the Story: Structure and Strategies in Contemporary Feminist Narratives* (Ithaca: Cornell University Press, 1989). Since her 1982 article, Judith Kegan Gardiner has written more extensively on Rhys, in *Rhys, Stead and Lessing and the Politics of Empathy* (Bloomington: Indiana University Press, 1989).

19. See also Jean Neide Ashcom, 'Two Modernisms: the Novels of Jean Rhys', in the *Jean Rhys Review*, 2:2 (1988).

20. Rose, 11.

CHAPTER 3. WRITING IN THE MARGINS

1. Howells, 14–17.

2. Mellown, 'Characters and Themes in the Novels of Jean Rhys', in Frickey, 106.

3. Gayatri Spivak, 'Three Women's Texts and a Critique of Colonialism', in Catherine Belsey and Jane Moore (eds.), *The Feminist Reader: Essays in Gender and the Politics of Literary Criticism* (London: Macmillan,

1989), 183.

4. Introduction, Belsey and Moore, 19.
5. *Spectator* 219 (21 July 1967), quoted in Mellown, *Jean Rhys*, 77–8: he makes the same comment again in 'The Return of Jean Rhys', in the *Caribbean Quarterly*, 16:4 (1970), 43–6.
6. Homi Bhabha, *The Location of Culture* (London: Routledge, 1994), 9 and *passim*.
7. Stuart Hall, 'Minimal Selves', in *The Real Me: Postmodernism and the Question of Identity*, ICA Document 6, (London: Institute of Contemporary Arts, 1987), 44.
8. Chambers, 23.
9. Howells, 5–6.
10. Zygmunt Bauman, *Modernity and Ambivalence* (Oxford: Polity Press, 1991), 4n. For Bauman modernity is both Enlightenment thought and modern industrial society: modernism, of course, is the artistic movement.
11. Rachel Blau DuPlessis has argued that all modernist women move towards postmodernism: see *The Pink Guitar*, 17.

CHAPTER 4. AUTOBIOGRAPHY AND AMBIVALENCE

1. Bauman, 56 and 45.
2. Bauman, 55.
3. Bauman, 183.
4. Bauman, 155–6.
5. Bauman, 156.
6. DuPlessis, *The Pink Guitar*, 42–3.
7. DuPlessis, *H.D.: the Career of that Struggle* (Brighton: Harvester, 1986).
8. DuPlessis, *The Pink Guitar*, 14. DuPlessis's quotations here are from Raymond Williams.
9. Whitney Chadwick, *Women Artists and the Surrealist Movement* (London: Thames and Hudson, 1985), 74.
10. Homi Bhabha, 11.

CHAPTER 5. THE DAY THEY BURNED THE BOOKS

1. Rhys was kept in touch with events in Dominica and the moves towards independence by her friend Phyllis Allfrey, author of the novel *The Orchid House* and later a minister in the short-lived West Indian Federation. Rhys got to know Allfrey in London in the thirties, and continued to correspond with her after her return to Dominica in 1953. See Emery, 19.

2. Frantz Fanon, *The Wretched of the Earth* (1965; Harmondsworth: Penguin, 1967), 28.
3. *Fort Comme La Mort* (originally published 1899) has been translated into English by Marjorie Laurie as *The Master Passion* and by T. E. Comba as *Strong as Death*. The mother and daughter central to this story are called Anne and Annette, suggestive of the names of Rhys's white Creole women (Anna, Annette, Antoinette). There is a fire here too – the burning of love letters, also marking the end of a relationship.

CHAPTER 6. *FORT COMME LA MORT*: THE FRENCH CONNECTION

1. *Saturday Review*, 23 April 1927, in Mellown, Jean Rhys, p. 4.
2. The presentation of the onset of madness in Maupassant's stories through a tense, divided, self-questioning narrator has much in common with Rhys's technique: the use of the fire in Maupassant's most famous story of madness, 'La Hurla', may be one additional influence on *Wide Sargasso Sea*.
3. Peter Hulme also makes this comparison, with a slightly different emphasis, in 'The Locked Heart'.
4. Chronotope is a Bahktinian term, particularly well defined by James Clifford as 'a setting or scene organizing time and space in representable whole form'. See his essay, one of the key texts in recent discussions of hybridity and diaspora, 'Traveling Cultures', in *Cultural Studies*, ed. by Lawrence Grossberg, Cary Nelson and Paula A. Treichler (New York and London: Routledge, 1992), 101. Clifford's example of a chronotope for the modernist period is the hotel – very apt for Rhys's work.
5. Gilroy, 202.
6. Gilroy, 221.
7. O'Connor, 2.

CHAPTER 7: THE POLITICS OF *GOOD MORNING, MIDNIGHT*

1. In French, *l'amour* and *la mort* are of course almost homophones.
2. Cf. the fictional Francine in *Voyage in the Dark*, and the historical Francine in *Smile Please*.
3. Tiffin, 328.
4. Bowlby, 41–4.

5. Ramchand, Introduction, *Tales*, no page numbers. Ramchand does point out that a similar atmosphere is found in Rhys's continental fiction: 'In the stories set in the Caribbean we find the soil of the rumour, gossip, innuendo, hypocrisy and malice of which the Rhys heroine remains acutely conscious even in the non-Caribbean stories'.

6. Of her other continental writing, her wartime stories are particularly tense and paranoiac, e.g. 'I Spy a Stranger', 'Temps Perdi', both first published in *Penguin Modern Stories* (London: Penguin, 1969) and 'The Insect World, (*TABL*).

7. Robert Young, *White Mythologies: Writing History and the West* (London: Routledge, 1990), 125. He is here drawing on Fanon and Césaire.

8. Douglas, *Purity and Danger: an Analysis of the Concepts of Pollution and Taboo* (London: Routledge & Kegan Paul, 1966), 104.

9. Douglas, 102.

10. Lucy Wilson has pointed out similarities between Foucault and Rhys in ' "Women Must Have Spunks": Jean Rhys's West Indian Outcasts', in Frickey, 73.

11. Emery, 144.

12. See Gardiner and Bowlby.

13. Virginia Woolf, *Three Guineas* (London: Hogarth Press, 1938), 186–7.

14. Angier talks about Lenglet's 'anarchic idealism': although it appears that she is referring to his temperament rather than his politics, his attitudes do sound like those of a political anarchist. (Angier, 369).

15. Romilly came to them after, among other eventualities, his expulsion for drunkenness from David Archer's left-wing bookshop in which he had earlier taken refuge.

16. I wonder how significant it was that Rhys found the advertisement in the left-wing *New Statesman* on the day it appeared. It could have been read by her third husband, Max, who, she said, was an ardent socialist who 'despises everything but majorities' and told her, clearly to her chagrin, that she was 'a High Tory' (*Letters*, 46). It certainly seems true that, while always 'on the side of the underdog', as Ford put it, she remained 'a savage individualist' (*Letters*, 275).

17. Like, as Shari Benstock points out, most women modernists and unlike most Anglo-American male modernists: Benstock, 31.

18. *Three Guineas*, 258.

CHAPTER 8. THE HUGE MACHINE OF LAW, ORDER AND RESPECTABILITY

1. Howells, 24. In Lacanian terms, the government and Mr Blank could

be said to represent the Symbolic Order, the Law of the Father, society's norms (and like Lacan, they would be sure there was only one symbolic order). How to fight society's ascriptions of meaning without being labelled insane, or even going insane, is one of the book's central concerns, as it is in all Jean Rhys's fiction.

2. The idea of patriarchy I have put forward in this paragraph – power in the hands of élite males, rather than all males – is of course what the word itself implies, though not always how it is used.

3. Harrison's examples are of moments when the protagonists talk back to men, but they talk back silently to empowered women too – take the case which I have just quoted of Inez Best in her women's ward.

CHAPTER 9. RESISTING THE MACHINE

1. Tiffin, 328–9. Although a number of critics have commented on mirrors in Rhys's work, there has been a tendency to see looking in a mirror as simply, in seventies feminist terms, slavery to the male gaze. Tiffin's postcolonialist perspective moves beyond this.

2 Juliet Mitchell, so influential in introducing Lacan's thoughts to feminism, presents in *Psychoanalysis and Feminism* (Harmondsworth: Penguin, 1974) a very negative view of the mirror image, an emphasis which has tended to stick in British appropriations of the concept. (Again, this could be linked with contemporary feminists' anxieties about enslavement to the mirror.) While of course the mirror image is a misrecognition, Lacan's own emphasis, in my reading, is, like Rhys's, on the image as enabling and necessary, even though lacking any kind of authenticity or essence. For a Lacanian reading of Rhys, though not, I found, a very convincing one, see Lori Lawson, 'Mirrors and Madness: a Lacanian Analysis of the Feminine Subject in *Wide Sargasso Sea*', *Jean Rhys Review*, 4:2, 1992. See too Ronnie Scharfman, 'Mirroring and Mothering in Simone Schwarz-Bart's *Pluie et Vent sur Télumée Miracle* and Jean Rhys' *Wide Sargasso Sea*', *Yale French Studies*, 62 (1981), 88–106.

3. Nancy Leigh draws attention to this splitting in her article 'Mirror, Mirror: the Development of Female Identity in Jean Rhys's Fiction', *World Literature Written in English*, 25:2 (Autumn 1985), pointing out that in *Voyage in the Dark*, 'Rhys makes it clear that Anna has divided herself into a self that acts and one that watches, inviolate and dispassionate. What the body does is held apart, so she can later think, "My mouth smiled" '. (p. 272); in 'Mixing Cocktails', Leigh picks out the narrator's bitter reference to those who feel that 'must interfere between your thoughts and yourself' (p. 283).

4. James Joyce, *Ulysses: the Corrected Text* (Harmondsworth: Penguin,

1986), 581.

5. 'Names matter', as Antoinette says (*WSS* 147). (Jean Rhys's own changes of names might merit study – something she has in common with an apparently very different novelist, George Eliot.) A fourth Russian comes up in Sasha's memories of the past – a macabre-minded man to whom she taught English before her son was born. Although she disliked him, it is with him she reads the words from Wilde I refer to later see (pp 65), words which certainly echo her own sentiments.

6. 'Most Russian and Spanish music means something to me. You see I like emotion – in fact am capable of *wallowing* in it. Adore negro music for example. It's life according to my gospel' (JRL 45).

7. Bowlby, 56.

8. Bhabha, 18.

9. 'Theory', in Dorothy Parker, *Not So Deep As a Well: Collected Poems* (London: Hamish Hamilton, 1937), 152. This poem was earlier collected in *Sunset Song* which first appeared in 1928. The first three lines went 'Into love and out again. Thus I went and thus I go/ Spare your voice and hold your pen –' .

CHAPTER 10. THE ENEMY WITHIN

1. The poem is called 'Les Mains de Jeanne-Marie'. The lines which I have translated here are in French 'Leur chair chante des Marseillaises/ Et jamais Eleisons', *Rimbaud: Collected Poems*, ed. Oliver Bernard (Harmondsworth: Penguin, 1962), 138.

2. The 'father' shouting 'murder' in the first dream in *Good Morning, Midnight* is perhaps expressive of this imbrication of feelings of oppression and aggression (*GMM* 12–13).

3. Vincent Descombes, *Modern French Philosophy*, trans. L. Scott-Fox and J. M. Harding (Cambridge: Cambridge University Press, 1980), p. 14.

4. Julia Kristeva, *Powers of Horror: An Essay on Abjection*, trans. Louis S. Roudiez (New York: Columbia University Press, 1982), 4. Kloepfler has used Kristevan ideas of the semiotic and symbolic in her work on Rhys, but although they lead her to some perceptive comments on textual detail, overall her approach is, I feel, reductively narrow.

5. *Powers of Horror*, 10.

6. *Powers of Horror*, 181.

7. *Powers of Horror*, 4.

8. Kristeva herself describes the deject ('the one by whom the abject exists') as an exile who asks *'where* am I?' rather than *'who*?', *Powers of Horror*, 8.

9. O'Connor has analysed the interlocking of these losses in *Voyage in*

the Dark (Jean Rhys, ch. 4, pp. 86–131).

CHAPTER 11. GOOD NIGHT, DAY

1. Bearing in mind the links Rhys makes between different kinds of oppression in the novel, it is perhaps significant that it is at the line from the negro spiritual that Sasha's defiance turns to despair.
2. Hélène Cixous and Catherine Clément, *The Newly Born Woman*, trans. Betsy Wing (Manchester: Manchester University Press, 1986), 76.
3. See note 12 to chapter 1. Helen Tiffin has an excellent discussion of Rhys's imagery of caging, enslavement and confinement, and points out the parallels such imagery highlights between characters like Marya and Lois, or Julia and Norah.
4. Paula Le Gallez, *The Rhys Woman* (Basingstoke: Macmillan, 1990), ch. 5, 'Sasha in Narrative Control', 114–140.

CHAPTER 12. THE STRUGGLE FOR THE SIGN

1. Gayatri Spivak, 'Reading the Satanic Verses', *Third Text*, 11 (1990), 41.
2. The surprising lack of critical comment on Rhys's comedy has been discussed recently by Katherine Streip, 'Just a Cérébrale: Jean Rhys, Women's Humour and Ressentiment', *Representations*, 45 (Winter 1994).
3. There are also, for example, the vacant masks which the powerless try to hide behind for protection: 'Isn't there something you can do so that nobody looks at you or sees you? Of course, you must make your mind vacant, neutral, then your face also becomes vacant, neutral – you are invisible' (*GMM* 17).
4. *Powers of Horror*, 45.
5. Hélène Cixous, 'The Laugh of the Medusa', in *New French Feminisms*, ed. Elaine Marks and Isabelle Coutevron (Brighton: Harvester, 1981), 249.
6. O'Connor, 1.
7. Cantwell, in Frickey, 24. This is the same interview referenced in note 6 to chapter 1. When it originally appeared in *Mademoiselle* it was entitled, in the wake of Alvarez's blessing, 'A conversation with Jean Rhys, "the best living novelist"'.
8. Frickey, 24.
9. She makes a similar point in the Ropemaker's Diary. 'I do not know "everyone". I only know myself' (*SP* 161). This seems to me a profound truth about the human condition, and one often stressed by modernists, but it has been interpreted as a symptom of Rhys's

personal egoism (Angier 462–4). Following Judith Kegan Gardiner's approach, one might point out that when T. S. Eliot says something similar, it is respectfully noted that he had studied F. H. Bradley's philosophy.

10. Julia Kristeva, 'The Adolescent Novel', in *Abjection, Melancholia and Love in the Work of Julia Kristeva*, ed. John Fletcher and Andrew Benjamin (London: Routledge, 1991), 10 and 8.

11. The French quotation, Marya says, is from Gauguin.

12. As Sue Roe says, 'the narrative of recollection is woven together with the more polished, stylised narrative of events, enabling the heroines to experience a collision of time schemes which enables the emergence of a particular symbolic imagery' (Roe, 240).

13. James, *Jean Rhys*, 62.

14. This clearly was not the case in the Bromley courtroom.

15. There are perhaps parallels with Virginia Woolf's later work. Gillian Beer has pointed out the extension of the use of speech and fragmentation in Woolf's final, eve-of-war novel, *Between the Acts*, where, as Beer says, 'Things broken apart, or lightly laid alongside, must take the place of fusion. Heteroglossia is here acted out by recording steadily what's thought, what's said, what's scrappily overheard' (Introduction, *Between the Acts*, London: Penguin, 1992, p. xiii).

16. Paul Theroux, quoted in Mellown, *Jean Rhys*, 31. The debate about Rhys's place goes on. As this book goes to press, Kamau Brathwaite has published an article in *Wasafiri*, 22 (Autumn 1995), 'A Post-Cautionary Tale of the Helen of Our Wars', attacking Hulme's article 'The Place of *Wide Sargasso Sea*': Brathwaite says that his position has been misinterpreted, that it is important to see Rhys as a Caribbean writer, but one must remember she is a Miranda not a Caliban.

Select Bibliography

BIBLIOGRAPHY

Mellown, Elgin W., *Jean Rhys: a Descriptive and Annotated Bibliography of Works and Criticism* (New York and London: Garland Publishing, 1984).

WORKS BY JEAN RHYS

'Vienne', *transatlantic review*, 2:2 (1924), 639–45; reprinted in *The Gender of Modernism*, ed. Bonnie Kline Scott (Bloomington and Indianapolis: Indiana University Press, 1990).

The Left Bank and Other Stories (London: Jonathan Cape, 1927); Short Stories Index Reprint Series, Books for Libraries Press (New York: Arno, 1970).

Quartet, first published as *Postures* (London: Chatto & Windus, 1928); reissued as *Quartet* (London: Andre Deutsch, 1969; Harmondsworth: Penguin, 1973).

After Leaving Mr Mackenzie (London: Jonathan Cape, 1930; reissued London: Andre Deutsch, 1969; Harmondsworth: Penguin, 1971).

Voyage in the Dark (London: Constable, 1934; reissued London: Andre Deutsch, 1967; Harmondsworth: Penguin, 1969).

Good Morning, Midnight (London: Constable, 1939; reissued London: Andre Deutsch, 1967; Harmondsworth: Penguin, 1969).

Wide Sargasso Sea (London: Andre Deutsch, 1966; Harmondsworth: Penguin, 1968).

Tigers are Better-Looking (London: Andre Deutsch, 1968; Harmondsworth: Penguin, 1972. Collection of short stories, some of which had previously appeared in *The Left Bank*.

'Temps Perdi' and 'I Spy a Stranger', in *Penguin Modern Stories* (London: Penguin, 1969); 'Temps Perdi' reprinted in *Tales of the Wide Caribbean*, ed. Kenneth Ramchand, and in *The Collected Short Stories* (New York: W. W. Norton & Co., 1987).

My Day (three autobiographical pieces) (New York: Frank Hallman, 1975).

Sleep It Off Lady (London: Andre Deutsch, 1976; Harmondsworth: Penguin, 1979).

'Making Bricks without Straw', first published in *Harper's Quarterly*, July 1978, in *Critical Perspectives on Jean Rhys*, ed. Pierrette Frickey (Washington, DC: Three Continents Press, 1990).

Smile Please, published posthumously (London: Andre Deutsch, 1979; Harmondsworth: Penguin, 1981).

Letters, 1931 – 1966, sel. and ed. Francis Wyndham and Diana Melly (London: Andre Deutsch, 1984; Harmondsworth: Penguin, 1985).

The Collected Short Stories (New York: W. W. Norton & Co., 1987).

Tales of the Wide Caribbean, ed. Kenneth Ramchand (London & Kingston, Jamaica: Heinemann, 1985).

Translations by Jean Rhys

Perversity, by Francis Carco, trans. (sic) Ford Madox Ford (Chicago: Pascal Covici, 1928); trans. credited to Jean Rhys (Berkeley, CA: Black Lizard Books).

Barred, by Edouard de Nève – nom de plume of Jean Lenglet, (Desmond Harmsworth, 1932).

BIOGRAPHICAL AND CRITICAL STUDIES

Abel, Elizabeth, 'Women and Schizophrenia: the Fiction of Jean Rhys', *Contemporary Literature*, 20 (Spring 1979), 155–77. Draws on the work of R. D. Laing.

Abruna, Laura Niesen de, 'Jean Rhys's Feminism: Theory against Practice', *World Literature Written in English* 28:2 (1988), 326–36.

Alvarez, Al, 'The Best Living Novelist', *New York Times Review of Books*, 17 March 1974, 6–7. For all its limitations, a crucial document in re-establishing Rhys's reputation as a writer.

Angier, Carole, *Jean Rhys* (London: Andre Deutsch, 1990). Extensively researched, with much new information, but apt to read the fiction too literally as biographical evidence.

Ashcom, Jean Neide, 'Two Modernisms: the Novels of Jean Rhys', in *Jean Rhys Review*, 2:2 (1988). An article which sets Rhys's thirties writing illuminatingly in the context of thirties modernism.

Belsey, Catherine, and Jane Moore (eds.), *The Feminist Reader: Essays in Gender and the Politics of Literary Criticism* (London: Macmillan, 1989).

Benstock, Shari, *Women of the Left Bank: Paris 1900–1940* (London: Virago, 1987).

Braybrooke, Neville, 'The Return of Jean Rhys', *Caribbean Quarterly*, 16:4 (1970), 43–6.

Bowlby, Rachel, 'The Impasse', in *Still Crazy After All These Years* (London: Routledge, 1993). Subtle reading of Rhys's modernism.

Campbell, Elaine, 'A Report from Dominica, BWI', in *World Literature Written in English*, 17 (April 1978), 305–16. Compares *Wide Sargasso Sea* with *The Orchid House*, the novel by Rhys's friend and fellow Dominican, Phyllis Allfrey.

—— 'Reflections of Obeah in Jean Rhys's Fiction' *Kunapipi*, 4:3 (1974), 340–9, reprinted in Frickey.

Cantwell, Mary, 'A Conversation with Jean Rhys, "the best English novelist"', *Mademoiselle*, 79 (October 1974), reprinted as 'A Conversation with Jean Rhys' in Frickey.

Casey, Nancy, 'Study in the Alienation of a Creole Woman: Jean Rhys's Voyage in the Dark', *Caribbean Quarterly*, 19 (September 1973), 95–102. Takes Rhys seriously as a Caribbean writer, but in spite of its title, not a particularly feminist account.

Emery, Mary-Lou, *Jean Rhys at 'World's End': Novels of Colonial and Sexual Exile* (Austin: University of Texas Press, 1990). Fruitfully brings together feminist, Caribbean and modernist approaches.

Frickey, Pierrette, (ed.), *Critical Perspectives on Jean Rhys* (Washington DC: Three Continents Press, 1990). Worthwhile collection.

Gardiner, Judith Kegan, 'Good Morning, Midnight; Good Night, Modernism', *Boundary 2*, 11 (Fall–Winter 1982–3), 233–52. Important step forward in the recognition of Rhys as a reading writer.

—— *Rhys, Stead and Lessing and the Politics of Empathy* (Bloomington: Indiana University Press, 1989).

Hagley, Carol R., 'Ageing in the Fiction of Jean Rhys', *World Literature Written in English*, 28:1 (1988), 115–25. Points out that women are not the sole victims in Rhys's novels.

Harris, Wilson, 'Carnival of Psyche: Jean Rhys's Wide Sargasso Sea', *Kunapipi*, 2:2 (1980), 142–50. Suggestive and poetic response by a fellow Caribbean modernist.

Harrison, Nancy, *Jean Rhys and the Novel as Women's Text* (Chapel Hill and London: University of North Carolina Press, 1988). Good on the feminist implications of Rhys's work.

Hearne, John, 'The Wide Sargasso Sea: a West Indian Reflection', in *Cornhill Magazine*, 1080 (Summer 1974), 323–33.

Hite, Molly, 'Writing in the Margins: Jean Rhys', in her book *The Other Side of the Story: Structures and Strategies in Contemporary Feminist Narratives* (Ithaca: Cornell University Press, 1989), ch. 1, pp. 21–54.

Howells, Coral Ann, *Jean Rhys* (London: Harvester Wheatsheaf, 1991). Clear, sensible introduction, looking at feminist, Caribbean and modernist approaches to Rhys. Good bibliography.

Hulme, Peter, 'The Locked Heart: the Creole Family Romance of *Wide Sargasso Sea*, in *Colonial Discourse/Postcolonial Theory*, ed. Francis Barker, Peter Hulme and Margaret Iversen (Manchester and New York: Manchester University Press, 1994), 72–8.

—— 'The Place of *Wide Sargasso Sea*', *Wasafiri*, 20, (Autumn 1994). These two articles give the most nuanced and comprehensive account so far of the debate about Rhys's place in a Caribbean tradition and the complexities ascribing the label West Indian to her work.

James, Louis, *Jean Rhys* (London: Longman, 1978). In spite of the uncertainty of biographical information at the time, remains a fine introduction to her fiction. James points to important areas that still need more investigation: the imagery of the social 'machine', and the influence of the music-hall on her art, which, along with the role of popular song more generally, is something still to be looked at. He does, however, read her work as more simply autobiographical than it now seems.

—— 'Sun fire – Painted Fire: Jean Rhys as a Caribbean Novelist', *Ariel*, 8:3 (1977), 111–127, reprinted in Frickey.

Kloepfler, Deborah Kelly, *The Unspeakable Mother: Forbidden Discourse in Jean Rhys and HD* (Ithaca and London: Cornell University Press, 1989). Influenced by certain Kristevan ideas, and, though narrow in focus, interesting on mothers and textuality.

Lawson, Lori, 'Mirrors and Madness: a Lacanian Analysis of the Feminine Subject in *Wide Sargasso Sea*', *Jean Rhys Review*, 4:2, (1991).

Le Gallez, Paula, *The Rhys Woman* (Basingstoke: Macmillan, 1990). Some illuminating comments on Rhys's narrative strategies.

Leigh, Nancy, 'Mirror, Mirror: the Development of Female Identity in Jean Rhys's Fiction', *World Literature Written in English*, 25:2 (Autumn 1985), 270–85.

Look Lai, Wally, 'The Road to Thornfield Hall: An Analysis of *Wide Sargasso Sea*', in *New Beacon Reviews: Collection One*, ed. John La Rose (London: New Beacon Books, 1968). First article to look at *Wide Sargasso Sea* as a Caribbean text.

Mezei, Kathy, ' "And It Kept Its Secret": Narration, Memory and Madness in Jean Rhys's *Wide Sargasso Sea*', *Critique*, 28:4 (1987), 195–209.

Mellown, Elgin, 'Characters and Themes in the Novels of Jean Rhys', in Frickey.

Miles, Rosalind, *The Fiction of Sex: Themes and Function of Sex Difference in the Modern Novel*, (London: Vision Press, 1974).

Naipaul, V. S., 'Without a Dog's Chance', *New York Review of Books*, 18 May, 1972, reprinted in Frickey.

Nebeker, Helen, *Jean Rhys: Woman in Passage: a Critical Study of the Novels of Jean Rhys* (Montreal, Canada: Eden Press, 1981). First full-length feminist account of Rhys's work.

Nunez-Harrell, E., 'The Paradoxes of Belonging: The White West Indian Woman in Fiction', *Modern Fiction Studies*, 31:2 (1985), 281–93.

O'Connor, Teresa, *Jean Rhys: the West Indian Novels* (New York and London: New York University Press, 1986). Richly perceptive account.

Plante, David, *Difficult Women: a Memoir of Three* (London: Gollancz, 1983).

Raiskin, Judith, 'Jean Rhys: Creole Writing and Strategies of Reading', *Ariel*, 22:4 (1991), 51–67.

Ramchand, Kenneth, *The West Indian Novel and Its Background*, (London: Faber and Faber, 1970). This has a chapter devoted to three white West Indian novelists, one of whom is Jean Rhys.

Roe, Sue, 'The Shadow of Light: the Symbolic Underworld of Jean Rhys', in *Women Reading Women Writing*, ed. Sue Rose (Brighton: Harvester, 1987), 227–62. Sensitive and evocative of the sense of loss in Rhys's work.

Scharfman, Ronnie, 'Mirroring and Mothering in Simone Schwarz-Bart's *Pluie et Vent sur Télumée Miracle* and Jean Rhys' *Wide Sargasso Sea*', *Yale French Studies*, 62 (1981), 88–106.

Spivak, Gayatri, 'Three Women's Texts and a Critique of Colonialism', in Catherine Belsey and Jane Moore (eds.), *The Feminist Reader: Essays in Gender and the Politics of Literary Criticism* (London: Macmillan, 1989).

Staley, Thomas, F., *Jean Rhys: a Critical Study* (London: Macmillan, 1979).

Streip, Katherine, 'Just a Cérébrale: Jean Rhys, Women's Humour and Ressentiment', *Representations*, 45 (Winter 1994).

Thurman, Judith, 'The Mistress and the Mask: Jean Rhys's Fiction', *Ms*, 4 (January 1976), 50–2, 91.

Tiffin, Helen, 'Mirror and Mask: Colonial Motifs in the Novels of Jean Rhys', in *World Literature Written in English*, 17 (April 1978), 328–41. The first article to bring together colonial and feminist perspectives, pointing out that in her work 'The parallel between male/female relationships and imperial nation and underdog is obvious' (p. 329).

Wilson, Lucy, ' "Women Must Have Spunks": Jean Rhys's West Indian Outcasts', *Modern Fiction Studies*, 32:3 (1986) 439–48, reprinted in Frickey. Some new insights into the black women in Rhys's fiction.

Wolfe, Peter, *Jean Rhys* (Boston: Twayne Publishers, G. K. Hall, 1980).

OTHER WORKS MENTIONED IN THE TEXT

Alatas, Syed Hussein, *The Myth of the Lazy Native: a Study of the Image of the Malays, Filipinos and Javanese from the 16th to the 20th century and its function in the ideology of colonial capitalism* (London: Cass, 1977).

Bauman, Zygmunt, *Modernity and Ambivalence* (Oxford: Polity Press, 1991).

Beer, Gillian, 'Introduction to Virginia Woolf', *Between the Acts* (London: Penguin, 1992).

Bhabha, Homi, *The Location of Culture* (London: Routledge, 1994).

Carter, Angela, *The Magic Toyshop*, (1967; London: Virago, 1981).

—— *The Sadeian Woman* (London: Virago, 1979).

Chadwick, Whitney, *Women Artists and the Surrealist Movement* (London: Thames and Hudson, 1985).

Chambers, Iain, *Migrancy, Culture, Identity* (London: Routledge, 1994).

Clifford, James, 'Traveling Cultures', in *Cultural Studies*, ed. Lawrence Grossberg, Cary Nelson and Paula A. Treichler (New York and London: Routledge, 1992), 96–112.

Cixous, Hélène, 'The Laugh of the Medusa', in *New French Feminisms*, ed. Elaine Marks and Isabelle Coutevron (Brighton: Harvester, 1981).

Cixous, Hélène, and Catherine Clément, *The Newly Born Woman*, trans. Betsy Wing (Manchester: Manchester University Press, 1986).

Davidoff, Leonore, *The Best Circles: Society, Etiquette and the Season* (London: Croom Helm, 1986).

Descombes, Vincent, *Modern French Philosophy*, trans. L. Scott-Fox and J. M. Harding (Cambridge: Cambridge University Press, 1980).

Douglas, Mary, *Purity and Danger: an Analysis of the Concepts of Pollution and Taboo* (London: Routledge, and Kegan Paul, 1966).

DuPlessis, Rachel Blau, *H.D.: the Career of that Struggle* (Brighton: Harvester, 1986).

—— *The Pink Guitar: Writing as Feminist Practice* (London: Routledge, 1990).

—— *Writing Beyond the Ending: Narrative Strategies of Twentieth-Century Women Writers* (Bloomington: Indiana University Press, 1985).

Ellmann, Maud, *The Poetics of Impersonality: T. S. Eliot and Ezra Pound* (Brighton: Harvester, 1987).

Fanon, Frantz, *The Wretched of the Earth* (1965; Harmondsworth: Penguin, 1967), first published in French in 1961.

Gilbert, Sandra M., and Susan Gubar, *The Madwoman in the Attic* (New Haven: Yale University Press, 1979).

—— *No Man's Land: the Place of the Woman Writer in the Twentieth Century*, vol. 1 *The War of Words*, vol. 2 *Sexchanges*, vol. 3. *Letters from the Front* (New Haven: Yale University Press, 1988, 1989 & 1994).

Gilroy, Paul, *The Black Atlantic: Modernity and Double Consciousness* (London, Verso, 1993).

Hall, Stuart, 'Minimal Selves', in *The Real Me: Postmodernism and the Question of Identity*, ICA Document 6 (London: Institute of Contemporary Arts, 1987).

Joyce, James, *Ulysses: the Corrected Text* (Harmondsworth: Penguin, 1986).

Kabbani, Rana, *Europe's Myths of the Orient* (London: Pandora, 1986).

Kristeva, Julia, 'The Adolescent Novel', in *Abjection, Melancholia and Love in the Work of Julia Kristeva*, ed. John Fletcher and Andrew Benjamin (London: Routledge, 1991).

—— *Powers of Horror; An Essay on Abjection,* trans. Louis S. Roudiez (New York: Columbia University Press, 1982).

Mitchell, Juliet, *Psychoanalysis and Feminism* (Harmondsworth: Penguin, 1974).

Parker, Dorothy, 'Theory', in *Not So Deep As a Well: Collected Poems* (London: Hamish Hamilton, 1937), 152. This poem was earlier collected in *Sunset Song,* which first appeared in 1928.

Rimbaud: Collected Poems, ed. Oliver Bernard (Harmondsworth: Penguin, 1962).

Rose, Jacqueline, *The Haunting of Sylvia Plath* (London: Virago, 1991).

Spivak, Gayatri, 'Reading the Satanic Verses', *Third Text,* 11, (1990).

Voloshinov, V. N., *Marxism and the Philosophy of Language,* trans. Ladislav Matejka and I. R. Titunik (New York: Seminar Press, 1973).

Woolf, Virginia, *Three Guineas* (London: Hogarth Press, 1938).

Young, Robert, *White Mythologies: Writing History and the West,* (London: Routledge, 1990).

Index

WRITERS AND THEIR WORK

RECENT & FORTHCOMING TITLES

Title	Author
Aphra Behn	*Sue Wiseman*
Angela Carter	*Lorna Sage*
Children's Literature	*Kimberley Reynolds*
John Clare	*John Lucas*
Joseph Conrad	*Cedric Watts*
John Donne	*Stevie Davies*
Henry Fielding	*Jenny Uglow*
Elizabeth Gaskell	*Kate Flint*
William Golding	*Kevin McCarron*
Hamlet	*Ann Thompson & Neil Taylor*
David Hare	*Jeremy Ridgman*
Tony Harrison	*Joe Kelleher*
William Hazlitt	*J.B. Priestley; R.L. Brett (introduction by Michael Foot)*
George Herbert	*T.S. Eliot (introduction by Peter Porter)*
Henry James -	
The Later Writing	*Barbara Hardy*
King Lear	*Terence Hawkes*
Doris Lessing	*Elizabeth Maslen*
David Lodge	*Bernard Bergonzi*
Christopher Marlowe	*Thomas Healy*
Andrew Marvell	*Annabel Patterson*
Ian McEwan	*Kiernan Ryan*
Walter Pater	*Laurel Brake*
Jean Rhys	*Helen Carr*
Dorothy Richardson	*Carol Watts*
The Sensation Novel	*Lyn Pykett*
Edmund Spenser	*Colin Burrow*
Leo Tolstoy	*John Bayley*
Charlotte Yonge	*Alethea Hayter*

TITLES IN PREPARATION

Title	Author
Peter Ackroyd	*Susana Onega*
Antony and Cleopatra	*Ken Parker*
W.H. Auden	*Stan Smith*
Jane Austen	*Robert Clark*
Elizabeth Bowen	*Maud Ellmann*
Emily Brontë	*Stevie Davies*
A.S. Byatt	*Richard Todd*
Lord Byron	*J. Drummond Bone*
Geoffrey Chaucer	*Steve Ellis*
Caryl Churchill	*Elaine Aston*
S.T. Coleridge	*Stephen Bygrave*
Charles Dickens	*Rod Mengham*

TITLES IN PREPARATION